FIELD & STREAM

CAMPING GUIDE

CAMPING SKILLS YOU NEED

FIELD& STREAM

CAMPING GUIDE

CAMPING SKILLS YOU NEED

T. EDWARD NICKENS
AND THE EDITORS OF *FIELD & STREAM*

weldon**owen**

CONTENTS

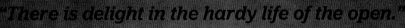

"*There is delight in the hardy life of the open.*"

—Theodore Roosevelt

Roughing It

It was at the end of a long, long day of fishing, at the end of a long, long week on the water. For six days we had portaged falls and paddled through rapids as northern Ontario's Allanwater River mutated from gentle stream to wind-frothed lake to plunging whitewater rapids and back again. Cruising through the skeletal forest burns, we'd watched sandhill cranes flying overhead. Rounding walls of lichen-crusted granite, we'd searched for pictographs and trailed a woodland caribou across the river.

Now the northern lights danced above our campsite, sending green and blue waves across a star-spangled black sky. I dragged a canoe to the edge of the water, climbed in, and set it adrift. A loon cried. My stomach bulged with pike and walleye. As I lay in the bottom of the boat, I could hear the purl of distant whitewater, the crackling of our campfire. This was our last night in the woods and every icon of boreal Canada—sky, fish, bird, water—was in cahoots to make it an unforgettable one.

Oddly enough, I've had that very feeling—that this is as good as it gets—many times, in campsites from Canada to Louisiana's Cajun country, from the wild shores of Alaska to the uninhabited barrier island beaches of the Carolina Outer Banks. Pair a hunting or fishing trip with a tent and a sleeping bag, or with a deep-woods cabin whose sooty windows are smudged with wood smoke, and every moment seems to be the best there ever was. Every trip is the trip of a lifetime.

Camping and outdoor sports do share a lot of common ground. Perhaps it's because of history: For untold centuries Native Americans gathered at prime fishing grounds, be they Pacific Northwest salmon rivers or the shad shoals of Southeastern streams. Entire villages struck their tepees and longhouses and wigwams to follow buffalo and elk and geese, a symbiotic migration that was as much about knowing how to pitch a perfect camp as knowing how to shoot a bird with an arrow. Perhaps the connection has to do with the visceral response of the human senses to yellow flames licking at a spitted fish or fowl. Or the fact that the best hunting and fishing

most frequently occurs in those places far from the madding crowd. Not to mention cell phones and computers.

For a host of reasons, a lot of folks can't conceive of taking a camping trip that doesn't involve a fishing rod. Or a hunting trip that doesn't end with a campfire and a cozy tent or backwoods cabin. If you're camping, you sack out mere steps from the pool where last night's white-fly hatch—and smallmouth bass—roiled the water. In the morning, you can lay out a cast while the coffee perks. I once shot a pair of wood ducks while standing on the edge of a sandbar campsite in my pajamas, not 15 feet from my frost-covered sleeping bag. You can't do that if you wake up at home.

But there are a lot of ways to go about sleeping on the ground, and not every camping trip requires you to give up all creature comforts. There's no question that backpacking into remote country is the epitome of the wilderness experience. Every decision—where to camp, when to rise, how long to fish, how far to trail the elk—is yours alone. In return for a tacit agreement to work with what the land and the weather offer, you have vespers of firelight and overhead stars. There might be planked salmon for supper and deer loin for breakfast. And then there are the people you meet in the backcountry: If you're lucky, there will be none of them.

Car camping, on the other hand, celebrates the best of both sides of the American travel spectrum—a little bit of Yellowstone, a little bit of Route 66. It's a fine way to find yourself in fish country. And let's be honest: Having a vehicle makes it much easier to restock the potato chip stash. Done well, with enough good-neighborliness and aluminum lawn chairs with dry-rotted seats, car camping is a great way to nudge into wild country.

And then there is *the* camp. The family fish camp. The friend-of-a-friend's hunting camp. The cabins and cottages at the end of the road, at the edge of the big woods, on the far side of the river. Maybe yours is merely a humble pile of bricks and boards. Maybe yours is a high-dollar getaway. Doesn't matter. What matters is the thing that all great hunting and fishing camps share: an accumulation of legend and lore, dusty window grime, and rusty cans of beans that turns a simple structure into a shrine.

The door's open. Kick off your boots. You must understand: You're walking on sacred ground.

So here's the trick. No matter your preference—whether a flat patch of ground 15 miles in or a deer camp beloved by your daddy and his daddy and his—most campers tend to fall into one of two, shall we say, camps. There is the Good Enough Camper who figures that just getting by is good enough. This type thinks this way: "It's only a couple of nights, so why do I need to pack an extra lighter?" This is the guy who forgets to bring any rope. He's the one whose tent always leaks, and the only thing weaker than his flashlight batteries are his excuses. And to make matters worse, this is the guy who's always borrowing your knife.

And then there's the guy who always seems to have the knots tied correctly and the fire banked properly—just in case. Part of it is knowing how, sure. But a big part of it is appreciating every moment in the woods and on the water as a gift. Who wants to be drying clothes by the fire when the trout are biting? Who wants to miss first light in the elk woods because you couldn't light wet wood? This guy always has the sharp knife. The right knot. The guylines taut as banjo strings. This guy has a name too: the Total Outdoorsman.

I want to be that guy. We all want to be that guy.

—*T. Edward Nickens*

1 PITCH CAMP LIKE A WOLF

Wild animals know how to pick the right spot to sleep. You'll know it, if you know what to look for. The perfect campsite is a blend of the haves and the have-nots. It should have a view that makes you want to leap from the tent and high-five the rising sun. Good water within 100 yards. It should be sheltered from the worst winds but not so cloistered that the skeeters like it, too. Give bonus points for rocks and logs that double as chairs. Double reward miles for a pair of trees that will anchor a tarp. The ground should not be squishy.

The wolf and the dog turn in circles before choosing a bed, possibly to scan for danger, and so should you, at least, metaphorically. Study overhead trees for "widow makers"—the dead branches that could fall during the night and crush or skewer the hapless camper. Pace off the ground that will be under the tent, clear it of rocks and roots, fill the divots with duff. Sleep with your head uphill and your heart filled with gratitude for the call of the cricket and the shuffling sounds of unseen feet beyond the firelight. —T.E.N.

2 TIE A CANOE TO YOUR RACKS

To tie down a canoe correctly, follow the rule of twos: two tie-downs across the boat, two bow anchors, and two stern anchors.

STEP 1 Place the boat on the canoe racks upside down and centered fore and aft. Tightly cinch the boat to the racks, using one cam-buckle strap per rack. Do not crisscross these tie-downs. It's critical to snug the tie-down straps or ropes directly against the gunwales where they cross under the racks.

STEP 2 Tie two ropes to the bow, and the end of each rope to a bumper. Repeat for stern anchors. Do not use the same rope or strap to create one long V-shaped anchor. Pad these lines wherever they run across a bumper edge.

STEP 3 Test the rig by grabbing the bow and shifting hard left, right, up, and down. You should be able to rock the entire car or truck without shifting the canoe. Do the same for the stern. Repeat after 10 minutes on the road and tighten if needed. —T.E.N.

FIELD & STREAM CRAZY-GOOD GRUB

3 MAKE A DUTCH OVEN CHICKEN QUESADILLA PIE

tight ring of coals

Dutch oven

6 to 8 coals

Making a one-pot meal in a Dutch oven is a campfire staple: It frees up the cook to sip whiskey and trade stories while pretending to be hard at work. This chicken quesadilla pie serves 10 to 12, and it's as easy as falling off the log you're sitting on while claiming to cook.

INGREDIENTS

5 lb. chicken breasts, cut into stir-fry–size chunks
2 medium sweet yellow onions, chopped
2 green peppers, chopped
1 large yellow squash, cubed
One 19-oz. can enchilada sauce
25 small corn tortillas
2 lb. shredded cheddar or jack cheese

One 16-oz. can corn kernels
One 16-oz. can black beans
3 boxes cornbread mix
3 eggs
1 cup milk

STEP 1 Sauté chicken, onions, green peppers, and squash until chicken is cooked through.

STEP 2 In a 14-inch Dutch oven, layer enchilada sauce, tortillas, cheese, canned ingredients, and cooked chicken-and-vegetables mixture.

STEP 3 Mix cornbread with eggs and milk according to box instructions and spread over the top.

STEP 4 Bake for 1 hour using 6 to 8 coals on the bottom and a tight ring of coals around the top.

—T.E.N.

4 MAKE A CAMP COFFEE CUP

Durn. You left your coffee mug at home again. But there's a tall can of beans in the camp cupboard and a hammer and tin snips in the shed. Get to it.

STEP 1 Remove the top of the can. Empty and wash the can.

STEP 2 Make a cut around the can's circumference (a) about 2 inches down; leave a vertical strip of can 1 inch wide.

STEP 3 Tap small folds over the sharp edges. Tamp them down smooth so you won't slice your lips.

STEP 4 Bend the strip down into a handle (b). Smirk at your buddies while you sip.
—T.E.N.

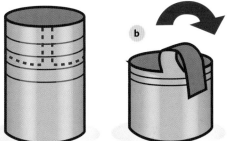

5 PUT UP A CAMP GUN RACK

Your guns are unloaded in camp—of course—but that still doesn't mean you want them leaning precariously against trees and walls. You can create an outdoor gun rack in 10 minutes with a sharp knife and two 5-foot lengths of rope.

STEP 1 Find or trim a downed branch about 6 to 7 feet long. It should have numerous smaller branches to serve as barrel stops; cut these to 2-inch lengths.

STEP 2 Select two trees free from branches to head height, about 5 feet apart.

STEP 3 Lash the support branch to the upright trees about 36 inches from the ground.

STEP 4 Institute a rule that all guns in camp must be placed in the camp gun rack. Violations are punishable by dish-washing and firewood-gathering duties. —T.E.N.

6 SHARPEN A HATCHET OR AXE IN THE FIELD

Assuming that you're savvy enough to have a file and whetstone in the toolbox, here's how to give your axe an edge.

STEP 1 Drive a peg into the ground. Place a wrist-thick stick 4 inches from the peg.

STEP 2 Place the poll of the axe against the peg, resting the cheek of the axe head on the stick so that the bit is very slightly raised. Rasp the file perpendicular to the edge and inward from the cutting edge to prevent burrs. Flip the axe and repeat on the other side.

STEP 3 Finish with a whetstone. Use a circular motion that pushes the stone into the blade. Flip the axe and repeat. —T.E.N.

head

poll

cheek

blade

edge

7 CUT THE CHEESE

Use a 12-inch section of one of the inner strands of parachute cord to slice cheese and salami when you leave your knife at home. —T.E.N.

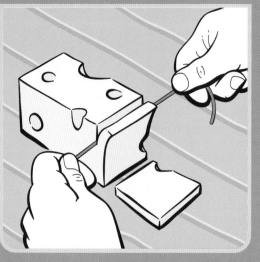

8 LIGHTEN YOUR PACK

2 TO 3 POUNDS Replace your leather wafflestompers with a pair of midcut boots with synthetic uppers.

½ POUND Ditch the flashlight for a lightweight headlamp. Some models offer both a long-burning LED for doing your camp chores and a high-intensity beam for nighttime navigation.

3 POUNDS Trade your tent for a tarp shelter. You can find some that weigh less than 2 pounds.

1 POUND Leave the hatchet at home; carry a wire saw instead.

2 POUNDS Cook with an ingenious wood-burning portable stove instead of a gas burner and avoid having to carry fuel.

1 TO 2 POUNDS Pack only two sets of clothes: one to wear around camp, the other specifically for hunting or fishing.

1 POUND Repack commercial food items in reclosable plastic bags and lightweight water bottles.

—T.E.N.

tarp shelter

portable stove

headlamp

synthetic boots

wire saw

water bottle

T-shirt

9 BE A BACKCOUNTRY BARISTA

Old-time cowboys wanted it thick enough to float a pistol and black as roofing tar. Here are three ways to brew the good stuff when you're miles (thank your lucky stars) from Starbucks.

RUGGED True cowboy coffee is about as simple as you can get. To make it, bring 2 quarts of water to a slow boil in a coffee pot. Remove it from the heat and add two handfuls of coffee, ground medium fine. Steep for 4 minutes. Settle the grounds with a splash of cold water or hold the coffee pot handle tightly and sling it once in an overhead circle. Some folks insist on adding crushed eggshells to settle the grounds.

REFINED A battered campfire percolator is a badge of honor, despite the fact that many coffee snobs snub the device because you have to boil the coffee. The secret is to use coarse-ground coffee and minimize boiling time. Use 1 to 1½ tablespoons of coffee for each 6-ounce cup and remove the percolator from the heat source as soon as the coffee color in the glass top meets your approval.

DANG-NEAR-FANCY Use a French press mug to brew seriously good backcountry joe the easy way. You can find 16-ounce presses that are perfect for camping. Pour 5 tablespoons of medium-ground coffee into the press, add 16 ounces of boiling water, and put on the top. Wait 3 to 4 minutes, slowly press the plunger to the bottom of the mug, and try not to smirk while you suck it down. —T.E.N.

10 ANCHOR A TENT IN THE SAND

It's always been a challenge to anchor a tent or a tarp on beaches, river sandbars, and other places where standard tent stakes won't hold because the ground is too loose or shifting. Finally, here's a solution for you: Bag it.

First, fill some garbage bags or empty stuff sacks with sand. Then tie a knot in each filled bag's opening. Tie the tent's stake loops and rain fly guylines to the bags to anchor them in place, and set the bags far enough away from the tent that the lines are pulled taut. If you're expecting high winds, you can take the extra precaution of burying the bags, which will provide a rock-solid stake point. To help batten down the hatches, add a few small sandbags along the inside tent edges. —T.E.N.

11 HANG FOOD FROM A TREE

You're not the only one out in the woods who's hungry. Bears, raccoons, coyotes, possums and lots of other critters will help themselves to any snacks you might leave in the open. Animals getting a taste for your treats is unsafe for you and them. Reduce the risk of losing your food by hanging it from a tall branch far away from the trunk.

STEP 1 Tie one end of a 40-foot length of parachute cord to the drawcord of a small stuff sack. Tie a loop in the other end of the cord and clip a small carabiner to it. Fill the sack with rocks and throw it over a branch that's at least 15 feet off the ground (a). Empty the sack afterward.

STEP 2 Clip the carabiner to the drawcord of your food storage bag, as shown (b). Run the sack end of the cord through the carabiner, and then pull on this end to begin lifting the bag off the ground. Keep pulling until the food bag is snug against the branch.

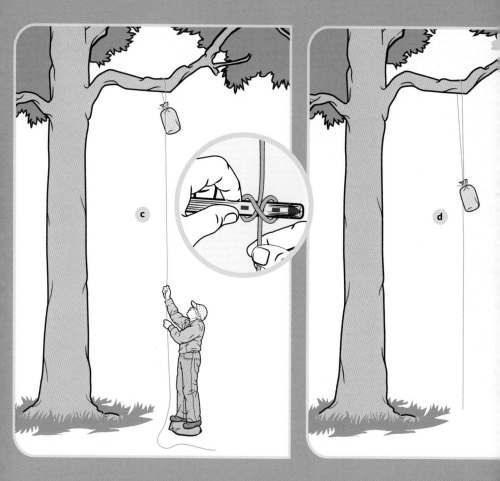

STEP 3 Find a sturdy twig and, reaching as high as possible, tie a clove hitch around the twig. Stand on a rock for additional height if possible. Slowly release the rock-sack end of the rope (c). The twig will catch on the carabiner to keep the food bag hanging (d).

STEP 4 When you need to retrieve your food, pull the rope down, remove the twig, and lower the bag. —T.E.N.

12 FIND HEAVEN ON EARTH

You've got to want to be here bad, to be here at all.

Since 1929, four generations of mostly Michigan hunters have trekked to Drummond Island's back-of-beyond Stevens Recreational Camp. First, they drive across the Mackinac Bridge, with Lake Huron to the right, Lake Michigan to the left. Then it's 60 miles to the eastern tip of the Upper Peninsula. Grab a ferry to Drummond Island and drive some more. Leave the hardtop maybe 8 miles west of the Canada border, then both hands on the wheel: Seven miles of logging road. One mile of rough trail through cedar thicket and birch woods, barely wide enough for a truck with the mirrors pulled in. For miles the woods are dark and deep. Then suddenly, an opening. There's a buck pole lashed to a pair of trees. Stacks of firewood. Kettle grills. A rough camp clinging to the edge of a cedar swamp. A welcoming curl of woodsmoke.

"It's agony to get here," says camp patriarch Ham Peltier. "But it's the Garden of Eden once you make it."

Peltier should know. He's hunted these big north woods for more than half of his 80 years. He knows all the places you'll never find on a map, but only in the memory of a Stevens Camp member. Pork Chop Hill and Slaughter Valley and the Cathedral. The Stone Pile, which is not to be confused with the Pile of Stones, which is not so far from the Stone in the Path. He knows every blind. Bear Den. The Office. The Boardroom. The Dumpster. And Ham's Perch, where Peltier has hunted for decades.

Peltier is the link to the deer camp's past. He remembers the sound of a sledgehammer banging an old tire rim that hung from a tree, a gong that brought home lost hunters. He remembers when you had to walk the last five miles in.

Things have changed a bit in recent years. These days, poker is played under propane lights. A small television and toaster run off car batteries. "Those old guys would turn over in their graves at all this newfangled stuff," says Chuck Decker, another steady hand at Stevens Camp. But this is hardly the Hilton. No showers. Brush your teeth with hot water heated in an old bean can. Ten bunks shoved into a bunkroom the width of a johnboat. A two-holer out back. "You love it or you hate it," Decker says. "There's no middle ground."

And they love it. To a man. Don Franklin is dressed in red and green wool plaid. He wears L.L. Bean boots. His belt holds an Old Timer sheath knife, 20 rounds of .30-06 ammo in a battered leather shell case, and an ancient Marble's No. 5 hatchet. He can show you the bones of the blind that his daddy hunted for 70 years.

"All year long," he says, small eyes misting, "a part of me never leaves this place." This is deer camp.

—T. Edward Nickens, *Field & Stream*, "Welcome to Deer Camp," October 2009

13 RAINPROOF ANY TENT

No matter how much money you doled out for your tent, you still need to take a few steps to make it rainproof. Too many campers fail to properly seal a high-tech shelter's numerous seams and then plop it down on an ill-fitted groundcloth and haphazardly stake out the rain fly. The result: soggy sleeping bags and long, miserable nights. From the floor to the fly, these three simple steps will ensure that you'll stay dry even in a sideways rain. Deal with them now—before the first drops start to land on your head.

SEAL SEAMS Tape-sealed seams, which look as if they have a narrow band of tape sewn in, require no sealing. All others on the floor and the fly do. Pitch the tent, turn the fly upside down, and stake it out tautly to open up the needle holes. Clean the seams with a cotton swab and household alcohol first. Seal tent-floor seams on the inside, so the sealant doesn't abrade off so easily in the field. Apply sealant with even strokes. Let dry for two hours and then reapply.

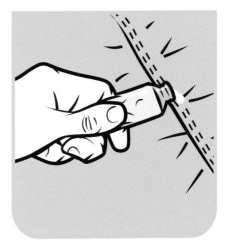

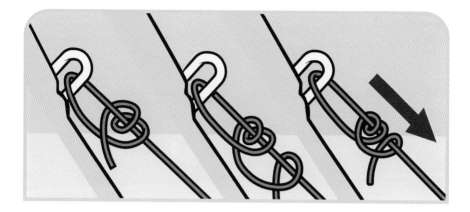

TIGHTEN LINES A rain fly works best when tightly pitched, which means you'll want those guylines pulled as taut as possible. The problem here is that your guylines will inevitably sag in the rain—and then you'll get soaked trying to retie them in a downpour. To avoid all of this, pregame by tying the guylines at home. Ideally, you are going to want to use reflective cord so that the lines are easy to work with in the dark. Out in the field, you'll be ready to attach the guylines to your tent's rain fly with a taut-line hitch knot (see above), which creates an adjustable loop that will allow you to increase tension quickly.

TIE IT DOWN Be sure to tie the knots onto the fly at the attachment points, not onto the tent stakes. This enables you to easily grab the guylines when you need to adjust them, instead of scrambling around in the dark trying to find the tent stakes and bent saplings that you used as anchors.

CUSTOMIZE YOUR GROUNDCLOTH
In the rain, a groundcloth keeps your tent floor from soaking up water. If the cloth extends beyond the edge of your shelter, however, it is going to actually catch rainwater and funnel it beneath your tent. Prevent this by tucking all of the groundcloth's protruding edges. Better yet, before you leave home, make a custom groundcloth. Set up the tent body (without the fly) outdoors on a piece of plastic or waterproof fabric. Stake it out and then trace the outline of the tent with a marker. Then you can strike the tent, and cut the plastic to 2 inches smaller than the outline you drew. Now no material will stick out from the edges to funnel rain under the floor. —T.E.N.

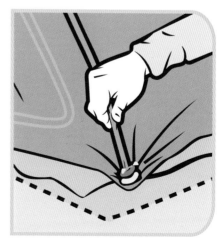

14 COOK FISH LIKE AN IRON ... ER, TINFOIL CHEF

Store-bought reflector ovens work wonders, but they're a little tricky to fit into a fishing vest. All it really takes to turn this morning's fresh catch into a memorable shore meal is a pocketknife and some heavy-duty aluminum foil. Reflector oven cooking is fast because you don't wait for glowing coals. It's easy because you can dress up a trout with whatever herb or spice is at hand. It's tasty because your fish is hot and smoky. And best of all, cleanup is as simple as wadding up the foil.

STEP 1 Cut yourself two branched sticks about 20 inches below the Y. Drive them into the ground at the edge of the fire ring, 18 inches apart. Wrap a 22-inch-long stick with heavy-duty aluminum foil, place it in the forks of the Y-sticks, and unroll foil at a 45-degree angle away from the fire to the ground. Anchor the foil with another stick and unroll a shelf of foil toward the fire. Tear off the foil. Place four dry rocks on the bottom of the shelf. These will hold any baking rack or pan.

STEP 2 To create the oven sides, wrap one of the upright Y-sticks with foil. Unroll the foil around the back of the oven. Tear off the foil. Repeat on the other side. Pinch the two pieces of foil together.

STEP 3 Build a hot fire with flames reaching at least to the top of the foil. You want a tall fire to reflect heat downward from the upper wall of foil. To broil fish, line a baking pan (or simply use the bottom shelf as the baking pan) with onion slices. Add the fillets, seasoned with lemon juice, salt, and pepper. An easy way to punch it up is to slather the fillet with store-bought chipotle sauce. Top with a few more onion slices. Flip once and cook until the fish flakes with a fork. —T.E.N.

15 CROSS OBSTRUCTIONS ON A CREEK

Blowdowns and beaver dams are common on many small streams, but they don't have to block your way to the fine fishing and hunting grounds that lie beyond them. Two paddlers in a canoe or johnboat can easily and safely cross such obstacles and stay as dry as toast—if they know how. With a little practice, you can accomplish this maneuver in two minutes or less.

STEP 1 As you approach the fallen log or beaver dam, secure any loose items—fishing rods, guns, daypacks—that will shift as you tilt the craft over the obstacle. If you're not wearing your life jacket, put it on.

STEP 2 Turn the boat parallel to the obstacle. One at a time, each paddler carefully steps out of the boat and onto the dam or log (a). Keeping a hand on the boat aids in stability. If the footing on a blowdown is particularly slippery, try straddling it. In streams with high flow, be very careful not to tilt the boat upstream or the water may catch the gunwale and flip it.

STEP 3 Face each other and then turn the boat perpendicular to the obstacle (b), with the bow between you. Lift the bow onto the log or dam. Work together to pull the boat up and over the obstacle.

STEP 4 Turn the boat parallel to the blowdown or beaver dam and board carefully (c). —T.E.N.

16 DRIVE AN ATV (ALMOST) ANYWHERE

The modern four-wheel all-terrain vehicle (ATV) is a great tool for hunters who want to get far from the pavement. But, as is the case with most tools for hunting, it takes more than a little skill to operate a quad safely. For most hunters, a good dose of common sense goes a long way, but even experienced riders can find themselves in precarious situations. If you go too fast over rough terrain or ask the machine to do something it wasn't designed to do, you're asking for trouble—and it will find you. Learn these five ATV driving skills, and you'll always be in control of your rig whether you're encountering unexpected obstacles or scaling the heights. —P.B.M.

LOAD UP Put oversize cargo—such as a field-dressed deer—on your rear rack, as close to the vehicle's center as possible. Setting a heavy load outside the frame can seriously compromise your ATV's maneuverability.

Once the load is centered, strap it firmly in place; rough ground can cause cargo to shift and impair handling. Use adjustable cargo straps rather than rope. Pick the least aggressive trail for the return trip and take your time getting back to base camp.

If your trophy is heavy enough to lift your quad's front end, forget about carrying it. Your only option is to drag it back to camp behind the machine.

WORK YOUR BRAKES As soon as you get on the vehicle, you should test the brakes to get a feel for their responsiveness. Always apply pressure to both the front and rear brakes as evenly as possible. Doing so helps ensure that you're always able to bring the ATV to a controlled stop.

If you cross through water deep enough to get the brakes wet, proceed with caution. The pads' performance will degrade until they dry. To speed this process, ride your brakes lightly to heat them up.

Fine gravel, mud, and the like can be very hard on your brake components. Rinse your ATV off after long rides to guard against mechanical failures.

CLIMB A STEEP HILL Newer quads are climbing marvels, but that doesn't mean you can forget about using common sense. When a steep hill looms, engage the lowest gear in four-wheel drive that's still capable of generating steady forward momentum.

Approach the hill straight on, stand, and move your weight as far forward as you possibly can without losing contact with the handlebar and foot controls. Cresting a sharp incline requires momentum, and that means speed.

At the same time, you don't want to goose the throttle halfway up. This can cause the wheels to spin, leading to a loss of control. If you can't make it up the hill safely, hit your brakes and set the parking brake. Carefully get off your quad and walk the rest of the way up the hill.

Anytime you sense that your ATV wants to take a tumble—whether heading up- or downhill—simply get off and let it go. It's not fun watching your machine roll down a slope, but it sure beats the alternative—you rolling with it.

RIDE OVER AN OBSTACLE Engage four-wheel drive and put your quad into a low gear. Approach the obstacle at a perpendicular angle and take it slow. Bear in mind that rocks and logs can move as you drive your ATV over them. The idea is to keep the rig balanced so it doesn't tip over. You may need to stand and shift your weight forward or rearward (or to the left or right) to maintain balance and see what's ahead of you as you're passing over the obstacle.

DESCEND A STEEP HILL Steep declines demand extreme caution. If a hill is both steep and muddy, you should just find an alternate route.

Downshift to your lowest gear in four-wheel drive. This way, the engine and transmission will help slow the ATV as you travel. You want to avoid stomping on the brakes, to avoid the risk of locking them up. If the brakes lock up, that can cause a slide

and loss of control. The idea is to feather your brakes intermittently—just enough to keep the descent safe and under your control.

Approach the drop head on. Lean as far back as you can while remaining in reach of your brakes; this weight shift helps keep rear wheels on the ground. Point your quad directly downhill. Turning off to the side could cause a rollover.

17 STAY WARM ON A COLD NIGHT

If you take care of your bag, your bag will take care of you: Each morning, spread your sleeping bag out in the sun to dry out any accumulated moisture. At day's end, fluff it up to restore its full loft as soon as you put up the tent. When it gets to be about a half hour before bedtime, toss a bottle of heated water down into the foot of your bag.

IN THE SACK You'll regret that one last mug of coffee around the campfire during your 2 a.m. bladder dash. Eat a snack to generate extra body heat from digestion and warm yourself up with a few jumping jacks. Pee right before you get into the tent. Zip your jacket around the foot of your sleeping bag. Tempting as it may be to cover your face with the edge of your bag in cold weather, it's better to sleep with your face exposed to reduce moisture accumulation from your breath.

IF YOU WAKE UP ANYWAY If you wake up cold, eat a small snack. If you have to go, go. Your body is wasting precious heat keeping all that liquid warm. Guys, you did remember the pee bottle, right? (Again, sorry, ladies.) —T.E.N.

18 MAKE A WICKED SLINGSHOT

Slingshot aficionados turn out sturdy handmade models capable of firing heavy slugs at 225 feet per second—fast enough to take game from squirrels to wild turkeys to ducks on the wing. Here's the drill on how you can craft the world's most awesome slingshot.

THE FRAME Dogwood, hickory, and oak will make the best frames. You don't have to look for the perfect Y-shaped fork. The typical right-hander will hold the slingshot in the left hand, so look for a fork where the main branch crooks to the left at 30 degrees or so, but a fork goes off to the right at about a 45-degree angle. Cut the frame and then let it dry for about three weeks.

THE POWER A number of companies sell ready-made replacement bands for slingshots. The trick lies in a strong connection. An inch and a half from the top of each slingshot "arm," drill a hole slightly smaller in diameter than the replacement band. Bevel the end of the band with scissors and thread it through the hole—a pair of hemostat clamps will make this easier. Snip off the bevel. Next, take a dried stick slightly larger in diameter than the inside diameter of the tubing and carve two half-inch-long stoppers to a point. Plug each end of the tubing with a stopper. —T.E.N.

19 TIE A BOWLINE KNOT

Forced to limit themselves to a single knot, most experts would choose the bowline (pronounced BOH-luhn), which is often called the King of Knots. The bowline has several magical properties. It is jam proof—meaning it unties easily no matter what kind of load it has been subjected to—and it is very secure. It also can be tied one-handed, making it the knot of choice should you find yourself adrift in the water with an unconscious buddy to rescue. A running bowline (a bowline in which you simply pull the standing end of the line back through the finished knot) creates a noose suitable for snaring game. Still, the real reason to learn it is that to seamen, fire and rescue personnel, and others who live and die by the rope, all humanity can be divided into those who know how to tie a bowline and those who don't. And it's always better to be on the side that's in the know.

STEP 1 Remember the phrase: *"The rabbit comes out of the hole, runs around the tree, and goes back in the hole."* Make an overhead loop in your rope (the rabbit hole) and pull the working end (the rabbit) through the loop from the underside.

STEP 2 Circle that working end behind the rope above the loop (the tree), and then back through it.

STEP 3 Pull to tighten. —B.H.

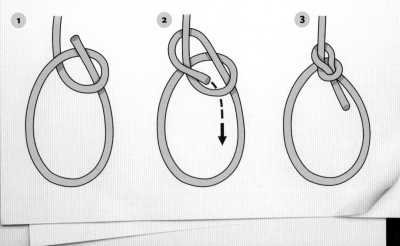

20 PEE IN A TENT

Nothing says "expert" like answering nature's call inside your tent. (Sorry, ladies. You're on your own here.) Here's the drill.

STEP 1 Roll over on your stomach. Place your pee bottle near the head of your sleeping bag. Sit up on your knees.

STEP 2 Shimmy the sleeping bag down to your knees. Lift one knee at a time and shove the bag below each knee. Your bag should be out of harm's way.

STEP 3 Do your thing. Afterward, thread the cap back on the bottle and store the bottle in a boot so it remains upright. Better safe than soggy. —T.E.N.

21 RATION AND REUSE FISH-FRYING OIL

You can reuse fish-frying oil several times during the same camping trip if you carefully strain it after cooking. Just carry an empty container the same size as the original oil bottle. After you fry the day's catch, let the oil cool, then strain it through a coffee filter into the empty container. After the next night's fish fry, filter the oil again by pouring it through another clean coffee filter into the original bottle. You can repeat the process several times. —T.E.N.

22 CUT PARACHUTE CORD WITH FRICTION

No knife? No problem. Tie the piece of parachute cord to be cut to two stout points—trees, truck bumpers, whatever. Leave plenty of slack. Take another few feet of cord (or the end of the line you're cutting if it's long enough) and place the middle of it over the piece of parachute cord to be cut. Grasp each end of this second piece, and pull firmly to keep tension on one spot. Saw back and forth, and the friction will melt the parachute cord right where you want it cut. —T.E.N.

23 SEASON A DUTCH OVEN

Dutch ovens can be hung over an open fire, buried in a pit of coals, and perched atop a gas grill or electric range. In the same Dutch oven you can fry fish, cook bacon, bake biscuits, and turn out the best apple fritters in the world. And absolutely nothing surpasses a Dutch oven for a lot of game cooking.

The secret is in the famous black pot patina. The surface of cast iron is rough and porous and will rust quickly. Seasoning a Dutch oven gives it a rust-proofing, nonstick, and flavor-enhancing coating that works better the more you use the pot.

DRIVE THE WATER OUT

Preheat a kitchen oven to 450 degrees F. Wash the Dutch oven with soapy, hot water, and rinse well. Put it in the oven for ten minutes.

BAKE THE FINISH ON

Remove the Dutch oven and let it cool. Turn your kitchen oven down to 300 degrees F. Now, grease the entire Dutch oven inside and out, including any and all lids and handles, with a light coating of cooking oil. Place it back in the oven for an hour. Crack a few kitchen windows and turn all smoke detectors off. It's going to smoke and smell like burned metal. Don't worry.

FINISHING TOUCH

Remove the Dutch oven and let it cool. Wipe away excess grease. Store with a paper towel inside. A newly seasoned Dutch oven will sport a shiny caramel color that turns black with use, especially if you cook bacon in it the first few times.

—T.E.N.

24 ENJOY A RIVER ENDING

I'm not sure I could devise a more perfect ending to a week in the Ozark wilds. It's our last night on the Eleven Point River, and the tents are up, and as the light falls, black-crowned night herons wing overhead to roost. My arms are sore from paddling four rivers, loading and unloading canoes, hauling bags over gravel bars, and casting tube jigs, Czech nymph rigs, and even a shrimp-colored spoon fly I offered to the Eleven Point when the storms came and the bite went flat after yesterday's breakfast.

Just downstream of our two-acre gravel bar campsite a hard current seam cleaves the river, with tendrils of fog swirling off the water like cigar smoke. Colby Lysne cinches down his belt and waves a flyrod. "This is the sword," he declares, "with which I will rule my kingdom."

I wave him off with a spatula.

For the next half-hour I trade rainbow trout and smallmouth bass nearly cast for cast, running back and forth between the river and a frying pan. Cast, strip, run, flip. Then suddenly, as if turning off a switch, it's over for me. I'm done. Fished out, plain and simple, after seven hard days on the water.

I lean my rod against the canoe and sprawl out on the ground, firelight flickering on Ozark stones, gnats pelting my face like a hard rain. A symphony of crickets trills in a chorus almost as loud as the sizzling fish, which are almost as loud as Lysne's cackle as he stands in the dark water, two-handing a trout. It's almost dark, and I can barely make him out in the fog, disappearing like some figure in a photograph that's faded in the sun.

A few stars wink overhead, and for the first time in a week I think about the fish and the fishing of days past, instead of plotting and planning and fretting about the fishing to come. I lie on the gravel bar, deep in the Ozarks, listening to the water that had taken all I had to give.

—T. Edward Nickens, *Field & Stream*, "Ozark Mountain Breakdown," June 2009

25 BUILD FOUR COOKING FIRES

In the same way that the proper ingredients make a recipe work, the right fire makes the cooking come together. The best backcountry camp cooks match the blaze to the dish. Here's how.

TEPEE FIRE If you need a steady, hot source of heat for a reflector oven or for roasting meat on a skewer, build a tepee fire of standing lengths of wood. Tall flames will produce the high-level heat required for even cooking. Keep plenty of small and medium-size pieces of wood ready to add to the fire for temperature regulation.

PINWHEEL FIRE To fry fish, you'll want a relatively small-diameter blaze closer to the ground, and one with precise temperature control. A pinwheel fire does the trick here. You can make one with 1- to 2-inch-diameter sticks of firewood laid out in a starburst pattern. Build it inside a ring of rocks or logs to hold the frying pan and feed the fire with dry wood to keep the oil roiling.

LOG CABIN FIRE The log cabin fire is made of a stack of crosshatched logs with an open center. This arrangement will provide lots of air circulation and plenty of wood surface for an even blaze. The result is a quick supply of cooking coals for a Dutch oven or foil-wrapped game.

KEYHOLE FIRE Multitask with a keyhole fire. Build a rock firepit in the shape of a keyhole. In the round part, build a tepee fire, whose tall flames provide both heat and light. In the narrow end, build a log cabin fire between the rock supports. The tepee will provide a constant source of coals once the log cabin fire burns down.
—T.E.N.

26 CREATE SHELTER WITH A TARP

If you have two utility tarps with grommeted edges, you can create the Taj Mahal of shelters, complete with a handy campfire vent hole.

STEP 1 Look for four trees in a rectangle and a fifth located between two of the others on the short side.

STEP 2 Tie a tarp between the four trees. The back edge should be about 3 feet off the ground, with the forward edge as high as you can reach. Call this the lower tarp.

STEP 3 Now tie the upper tarp in place. Be sure that you position it so that it slides under the forward edge of the lower tarp

by a couple of feet. Once it's in place, tie the side grommets together so that you create an open flap in the middle of the two tarps.

STEP 4 Tie a guyline from the middle of the back edge of the lower tarp to the fifth tree, cinching it tight. You now have a smoke vent.

STEP 5 Build a fire with a stacked-log back wall, and smoke will rise to the tarp roof and exit through the hole that you've created. —T.E.N.

27 CLEAR A DOWNED TREE WITH A CHAIN SAW

Before attempting to buck a fallen tree, take time to figure out the binding pressures. Next, clear out any saplings or branches that the downed tree has fallen on; these can spring up forcefully when pressure is released. Stand on the uphill side of the tree and come prepared with a few plastic wedges to keep the chain-saw bar from binding.

TREE FLAT ON THE GROUND Cut from the top. Don't let the chain touch the ground, which dulls the blade and can send shrapnel flying. Cut partway through the log, then either roll it to continue or lever it up from the bottom and shim it with a piece of wood.

TREE SUPPORTED AT ONE END
Make an initial cut from the bottom up, about one-third of the log's diameter. Finish with a second cut from the top down to meet the first.

TREE SUPPORTED AT BOTH ENDS
Make the first cut from the top down. Watch for binding, use wedges if need be. Then cut from the bottom up. —T.E.N.

28 TIE A BUTTERFLY LOOP

Tie this loop in the running part of a line and use it to hang gear, as a ladder step, or make a canoe bridle to tow a canoe behind a boat.

STEP 1 Hang a rope from your hand and coil it twice to form three coils (a). Move the right coil to the left, over the middle coil (b). The center coil now becomes the right coil.

STEP 2 Move this coil to the left over the top of the other two coils (c).

STEP 3 Take the coil you just moved to the left and pass it back to the right, under the remaining coils, to form a loop (d).

STEP 4 Pinch this loop against your palm, using your thumb to hold it. Slide your hand to the right, pulling this loop (e). Tighten the knot by pulling both ends of the rope (f). —T.E.N.

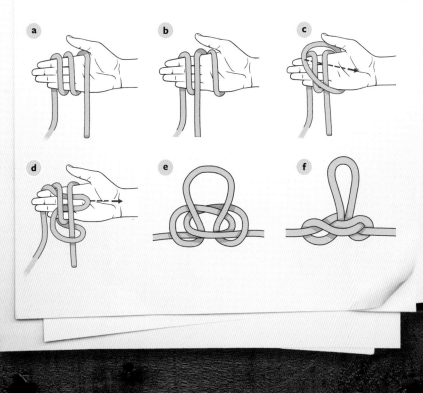

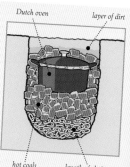

29 DIG A BEAN HOLE

Digging a bean hole is a storied tradition in the North Woods, but there's no reason you can't do it anywhere. The wood smoke and molasses flavors in this bean dish can't be duplicated any other way.

INGREDIENTS

10 cups dried Great Northern or yellow-eyed beans
1 lb salt pork, cut into 2-inch strips
2 large onions, diced
2 ½ cups molasses
4 tsp. dry hot mustard
2 tsp. black pepper
½ cup butter

STEP 1 Dig a hole that's twice as deep as and one foot in diameter larger than the Dutch oven you're planning to use. Next, toss a few rocks or a length of chain into the bottom of the hole. Fill the hole with hardwood and then burn the wood down until the hole is about three-quarters full of hot coals.

STEP 2 Over your open fire (or on a camp stove), precook the beans by slow-boiling them for about 30 minutes. Drain and set aside.

STEP 3 Place the salt pork in the Dutch oven, layer onions on top, and pour in the beans, molasses, mustard, and black pepper. Slice the butter and place on top. Add enough boiling water to cover the beans by ½ to 1 inch. Cover the pot with aluminum foil and then the lid.

STEP 4 Shovel out about a third of the coals and put the bean pot in the hole. Replace the coals around the sides and on top of the oven; fill the rest of the hole with dirt. Cooking time varies, but give it a good 8 hours. —T.E.N.

30 SIPHON GAS THE SAFE WAY

This method relies on physics to work. You need 6 feet of clear tube, a clean container for the gas, and possibly something to stand on.

STEP 1 Run the hose into the gas tank until the end of it is submerged. Blow gently into the hose and listen for gurgling noises to know you've found the liquid.

STEP 2 Form a loop in the tubing with the bottom touching the ground and the end rising to a level higher than the gas in the tank. It'll help to stand on something.

STEP 3 As you gently suck on the hose, watch the gas move to the bottom of the loop and start to rise. Stop sucking at this point; the gas should now come to the level of gas in the tank on its own.

STEP 4 Stick the tube's free end into a container and then slowly lower it to the ground. When you have enough, raise the container to a level higher than the gas tank. Remove the hose from the container and straighten it so excess gas reenters the tank. —T.E.N.

31 OPEN A BREW WITH A BLADE

Napoleon's soldiers were famous for opening champagne by slicing off the neck of the bottle with their sabers. If you want to be that impressive (if a little less fancy), you can open a beer bottle by slicing off the neck with a single blow from a cleaver—with practice.

Really, though, there's an easier and much safer method for getting into that nice cold brewski. First, hold the neck of the bottle tightly, with the top of your hand just under the bottom of the cap. Place the back of your knife blade across the top of the third knuckle of your index finger and wedge it under the edge of the cap. Pry up. —K.M.

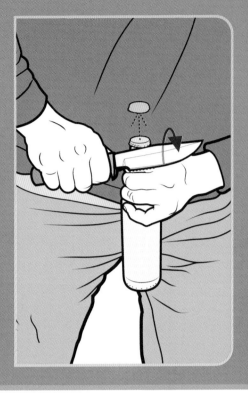

32 WHITTLE A WHISTLE OUT OF A STICK

Cut and peel the bark from a finger-length section of any stick with a soft pith, such as elder. Next, use a thin twig to bore out this pith, leaving a hollow cylinder (a). Cut a notch near one end (b). Whittle a smaller piece of wood that will fit snugly into the notch end and then slice a little off the top of that plug to allow for the passage of air (c). Fit the plug into the cylinder, trimming the end to shape (d). Place your finger in the other end and blow into the mouthpiece to force the air over the notch in the top of the whistle. When you get a clear whistle, the plug is well fitted. Permanently plug the end with a short piece of wood (e). —K.M.

a *Push or bore out the pith, leaving a hollow cylinder.*

b *Make a V notch on top.*

c *Cut a plug that fits into the cylinder and then slice off the top.*

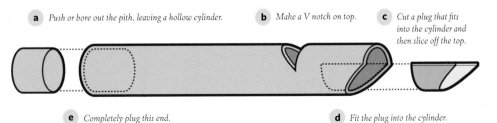

e *Completely plug this end.*

d *Fit the plug into the cylinder.*

33 BUTCHER A WET LOG

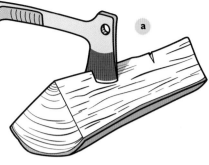

Forget searching for tinder fungus and belly-button lint to start your fire. With a hatchet, you can render fire-starting scrap from a wet log.

STEP 1 Find a solid log no more than 10 inches in diameter. A coniferous wood like pine or cedar works best due to its flammable resin. Cut a 12-inch section from the log.

STEP 2 Split the log into quarters. Lay one quarter on the ground, bark side down. Score the edge with two 1-inch-deep cuts, 4 inches apart (a). Shave thin 4-inch-long dry wood curls and splinters (b). Pound these curls with the back of the hatchet to break up the wood fibers and then rub some of these between your palms to separate the fibers further. This is your tinder; you'll need two handfuls.

STEP 3 Split pencil-size pieces from the wedge corners of a remaining quarter. Break these into 6-inch pieces for kindling.

STEP 4 Continue to split the quarters, utilizing the innermost and driest pieces. Use these as small and large pieces of fuel. —T.E.N.

34 BREAK WIND LIKE A COMMANDO

The occasional bout of morning thunder is as much a part of deer camp as five-card stud. Foster a universally appreciated rip with a combination of nuance and nerve.

AMBUSH Approach your pals with detached nonchalance and let fly with a drive-by toot. Go easy on the volume and vacate the premises promptly.

CAMO JOB Get the wind moving. Ruffle papers, stand by a fan. Light a cigar.

BLAME GAME Don't draw attention to yourself. Try a slight turn of the head and a softly muttered oath, followed by a rhetorical "Someone need a little private time?"

JUST THE TWO OF US If you're stuck in a car or tent with just one pal, name it and claim it, buddy. Be loud. Be proud. —T.E.N.

35 RECOVER A STUCK VEHICLE

Two difficult tasks await: summoning the courage to ask for help and getting your rig out of the soup without trashing the frame or maiming a bystander. You're on your own for getting help, but here's the step-by-step to follow once you do.

STEP 1 Clear the area around the wheels and differentials and then shovel out a trench in front of the wheels in the direction you need to move.

STEP 2 Shove floor mats, sticks, or sand under the wheels to help your vehicle get some traction.

STEP 3 Attach the tow strap to tow hooks, holes in the frame, or receiver hitches of your vehicle—and then to the other vehicle. Avoid attaching the strap to axles or anything else that moves. Don't use a trailer hitch ball as a recovery point. Share the tow load by using two tow points if possible.

STEP 4 Put both vehicles in four-wheel drive low, slowly pull out the slack in the strap, and bump up the RPMs in each vehicle. Pull in as straight a line as possible. If this doesn't work, have the tow vehicle back up a few feet and get a rolling start at 3 mph. —T.E.N.

36 FELL A TREE WITH A KNIFE

A knife isn't as good as an axe in the backcountry. But when you're lost in the woods and it's your only friend, you can do a lot with a sturdy sheath knife—including felling a tree for a wickiup frame or firewood.

STEP 1 FROE AND MALLET Using a stout fixed-blade knife, hold the blade horizontally against the tree, with the cutting edge pointing slightly downward. With a heavy stick, pound the blade into the trunk. Remove the blade, and make another cut with the blade turned slightly upward to remove a wedge of wood.

STEP 2 ROUND AND ROUND You need to completely girdle the tree this way. Don't bend it over until the cuts go all the way around, or you'll splinter the wood, which makes it harder to cut.

STEP 3 PUSH AND SHOVE Once you've cut all the way around, give the trunk a shove. If it doesn't budge, remove more wedges. —T.E.N.

37 BUILD A FIRE FOR MAXIMUM COOKING COALS

The perfect call, the perfect shot, your bull quarters are hanging like clean laundry, and it's time to eat. Don't blow it by rushing the fire. Building the perfect grilling fire takes about 45 minutes, but the results definitely make it worth the effort. Follow the steps below to be sure of success.

STEP 1 Look for woody debris in the form of dead lower limbs on standing lodgepole and whitebark pine trees. Break off limbs with plenty of brown needles still attached. Once you have enough, pile them up in the fire pit. The needles will serve as tinder, the twigs as kindling, and the branches are the beginning fuel to get your fire going.

STEP 2 You'll need 4 to 6 inches of glowing coals, so pile on the pine. Forgo the tepee-style fire for a crisscross log cabin setup that allows more air to circulate around larger pieces of wood. Burn pieces that are 4 to 6 inches in diameter and short enough so that each chunk of wood burns in its entirety at the same rate.

STEP 3 As the last of the pine flames die down to coals, it's time to pile on dead aspen limbs. These should be about 20 inches long and 3 to 4 inches in diameter. Once they burn down to coals, and no flames are visible, slap on the steaks. The aspen smoke turns a good elk steak into a meal to remember. —T.E.N.

38 MAKE WATERPROOF MATCHES

To make your own waterproof matches, use clear nail polish instead of paraffin wax. Nail polish is more durable and won't gunk up the match striker.

STEP 1 Fill a soft-drink bottle cap with nail polish (a).

STEP 2 Dip each match head into the polish (b) and then lay the match on the tabletop with its head extending off the edge (c). Repeat.

STEP 3 Once the polish has dried, hold each match by the head and dip the entire remaining wooden portion of the match into the nail polish bottle (d).

STEP 4 Place matches on wax paper to dry. —T.E.N.

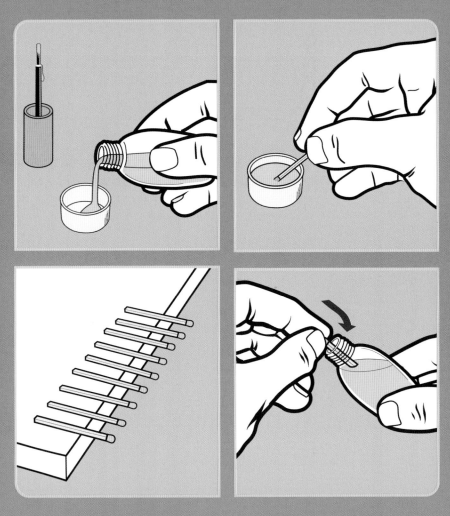

39 TWIST UP A CONSTRICTOR KNOT

Easy to tie and extremely reliable, the constrictor knot is one of the most useful knots on earth. It exerts a ratchetlike grip on any curved surface, such as a post, rail, tree, or human appendage. You can use it to close the mouths of food bags and gear bags large and small; make a whipping in string around the end of a larger rope, preventing the latter from fraying; secure a rod tube to a backpack; and fashion a string leash for your eyeglasses. Tie it around the snout of a bear after placing a hardwood stick through the jaws behind the fangs, and, with a noose over the nose and around the ends of the stick, you can tote the critter without ruffling its fur. To hang camp tools, file a rough groove in each tool's handle, tie a constrictor hitch around it, and then knot together the ends of the cord. The constrictor's virtues are, alas, also its only vice: It is not easily untied. Then again, it won't come undone accidentally, either.

STEP 1 Make a simple loop, crossing the working end of the rope over the other.

STEP 2 Circle the working end behind the item you're tying up then pass it under the standing end and under your "X."

STEP 3 Pull both ends to constrict. —B.H.

40 CHOOSE THE RIGHT KNIFE

No other tool is called upon to perform as many tasks, in as many ways, under as many conditions, as the knife. It can take a life and save one. Cut cord, open the belly of an elk, help spark a fire, and skin a fish. A good knife is a tool, an icon, a symbol of its bearer's take on what it takes to live well in the woods. And the know-how to use a sharp blade never goes out of style.
—T.E.N.

JIMPING Corrugated grooves in the blade spine, choil, or handle for increased grip and a no-slip feel.

SPINE The back of the blade, most often unsharpened and unground. A thick spine gives a knife strength.

FIXED BLADE KNIVES
are inherently strong due to the tang, the extension of the blade that carries into the knife handle. Also called sheath knives, fixed blades are easy to clean and quick to put into action. They have no moving parts to break or gunk up with hair, blood, or grit. And the sleek lines of a fixed blade knife speak to the essence of outdoors competence— simple elegance and deadly efficiency.

BELLY The curved arc as the sharpened edge nears the blade tip. A knife with a lot of belly will have a sagging, swooping profile, perfect for the sweeping cuts needed to skin big game.

CHOIL The unsharpened edge of the blade between the end of the handle and the beginning of the edge bevel. Many knives have a finger indent at the choil to aid in choking up on the blade.

THUMB RAMP An elevated hump on the spine of the blade near the handle. It provides increased control of the knife and reduced forearm fatigue during periods of extended use.

THUMB HOLE OR STUD
A hole in the spine or a stud that protrudes from the blade of a folding knife near the handle and allows the user to open the knife one-handed.

SPYDERCO
CPM-M4

GRIND The finished shape of the blade when viewed in cross section. There are two basic grinds. Hollow-grind blades have a concave shape and are easily sharpened, but tend to hang up in deep cuts. Flat-grind blades taper evenly from the spine to the cutting edge and hold an edge well.

RICASSO The shank of the blade between the handle and the beginning of the sharpened edge. The ricasso often carries the maker's identifying mark, or "tang stamp."

FOLDING BLADE KNIVES can be smaller and easier to carry than fixed blade models. Larger folding blades with pocket clips and strong locking mechanisms are hugely popular. Many are designed to be opened with one hand through the use of a thumb stud or blade hole, and some are built with assisted-opening devices that propel the blade into a fixed position after the user opens it partway.

THE SHAPE OF THINGS THAT CUT

The shape of a blade determines how well that blade will perform specific tasks. Depending on whether you are hunting or fishing, or even if you just need a basic all-around camping and survival knife, knowing these basic facts and terms will help you determine which knife is your best option.

CAPER A short, pointed blade with a slightly downturned tip is easy to control in tight spots, such as removing the cape from an animal's head.

RECURVE The slight S-shaped belly forces the material being cut into the sharp edge. Recurves can be designed into most blade profiles.

CLIP POINT The classic general-use blade in which the spine of the blade drops in a concave curve to the tip (the "clip") to make a strong piercing point with a slightly upswept belly.

FILLET A thin, flexible blade allows the fillet knife to be worked over and around bones and fins.

DROP POINT A downward convex curve along the blade spine forms a lowered point, which keeps the tip from cutting into an animal's organs during field dressing.

SKINNER The full curving knife belly is perfect for long, sweeping motions, such as skinning big game.

41 CAMP WITHOUT A TENT

Most modern tent rain flies can double as tarps, but there's nothing wrong with using a standard tarp as long as you make sure to pre-tie the guylines and follow this routine.

PREP AT HOME Attach two 18-inch guylines to each corner of the tarp. Attach 12-inch guylines to all other grommets. In the tarp's stuff sack, stash a 50-foot length of parachute cord for a ridgeline, another 10 sections of cord cut to 20-foot lengths for extra grommet ties, and 12 tent stakes in case there are no trees.

IN THE FIELD Once you're out in the woods, all your prep pays off. To create your lean-to-style shelter, start by tying a ridgeline to two trees. To attach the tarp, wrap one corner guyline clockwise a half-dozen times around the ridgeline and wind its mate counterclockwise a half-dozen times in the opposite direction. Connect them with a shoelace knot. Stretch the tarp out and repeat on the opposite corner. Tie the remaining guylines along this edge to the ridgeline. Then stake out the back and sides. Finally, erect a center pole to peak the tarp—if it rains, the droplets will run right off. —T.E.N.

42 MAKE A TWO-STEP BACKPACKER'S MEAL

End of the trail, end of the day—the last thing you want to do is channel some television chef over a hot fire. This backpacking meal requires nothing but a single pot, a handful of lightweight ingredients, and minimum cleanup. If you and your buddy take turns digging a spoon into the mix, you can skip plates altogether.

INGREDIENTS

One 6-oz. package of instant stuffing mix
3 tbsp. olive oil
12 sun-dried tomatoes
Two 3.5-oz. tins smoked oysters
One 8-oz. can water chestnuts

STEP 1 To a 2-quart pot, add the stuffing's required amount of water, plus 3 tablespoons.

STEP 2 Follow box directions for stuffing with these exceptions: (1) Replace butter with olive oil. (2) Toss in the sun-dried tomatoes and simmer for five minutes before adding stuffing mix. (3) After stuffing is ready, stir in oysters and water chestnuts. Mix thoroughly. —T.E.N.

43 ROAST THE PERFECT MARSHMALLOW

When you're roasting marshmallows, don't settle for ashy black marshmallow goo. Achieving the perfect balance of golden smokiness and creamy gooliciosity (that's a real word—you don't have to look it up) is no small feat, so let's get serious.

ONLY JET-PUFFED OR CAMPFIRE BRANDS WILL DO Many brands burn way too quickly. And only a chump uses a coat hanger as a skewer. Cut a straight roasting stick. No forked branches; no funky twigs. Keep it plain, straight, and simple. Hold the marshmallow level over embers, not flames. It's fine to have flames off to one side, but they shouldn't be directly under your precious glob of sugary wonderfulness. Rotate the marshmallow slowly, or go for a quarter turn at a time. (Here's where the straight stick comes into play: You don't have to change positions when you rotate it.)

WATCH FOR THE TELLTALE SAG As the marshmallow turns a tawny golden color, it will sag on the skewer. When a slit appears where the stick and marshmallow meet, you know the insides are approaching that state of gooliciosity. It is time. —T.E.N.

Toss around some nifty rope-work lingo to assure bystanders that you're a knothead of the first order. The *bitter end, tag end,* or *working end* is the end of the line that is being used to tie the knot. The *standing end* is the other end. A *bight* is a doubled section of rope that doesn't cross over itself. A *loop* is a bend in the rope that does. And a knot is, alas, not always just a knot. A *bend* is a knot that joins two lines together. A *hitch* is a knot that attaches a line to a rail, post, or another line. —T.E.N.

45 SHARPEN A KNIFE WITH A WHETSTONE

Stroking a knife blade against a whetstone is the most traditional sharpening method. With a flat stone—medium grained (300 grit) on one side and fine grained (600 grit) on the other—you can maintain a fair edge on a knife using spit to grease the stone and eyeballing a 20- to 30-degree angle, just the way Grandpa did. You'll get a more even edge by using a good-quality honing oil instead of just water to wet the stone and by wedging a coin or two under the spine of the blade to help establish the proper angle for sharpening before you start.

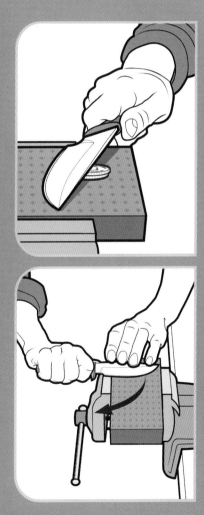

GET THE ANGLE With the whetstone in a vise, place one or two coins under the blade to establish the angle. Then remove the coins and sharpen at that angle. You can easily damage your stone if you keep the coins under the blade while sharpening.

SWEEP THE STONE Slide the knife across the stone in an arc, using even pressure. Use the same number of strokes on both sides of the knife's edge.

To resharpen a dull blade, start with 30 strokes on the stone's medium-grit side. Follow that step with 100 strokes on the stone's fine-grit side. —K.M.

46 PUT TOGETHER A HANDY REPAIR KIT

Tents tear, lantern mantles fade, zippers fall off track. Overcoming these and other breakdowns requires you to be equal measures seamstress and handyman. With a simple repair kit stowed in your truck or at deer camp, and the skills to fix anything, you'll be well armed to survive and thrive in the woods. Here's a good starting point, customize at will. —DAVID DRAPER

☐ Cable ties

☐ Shoe repair glue

☐ Waterproofing wax

☐ Duct tape

☐ Replacement zippers

☐ Sewing kit

☐ Spare buckles for all straps

☐ Washers

☐ Safety pins

☐ Replacement mantles

☐ Cord locks

☐ Tent repair kit

☐ Shock cord

☐ One-inch-wide webbing strap

☐ Tent pole splints

☐ Parachute cord

☐ Stove/lantern repair parts

47 REPLACE A BUSTED ZIPPER

A zipper that separates or won't close can usually be blamed on a broken slider. This can often be fixed by gently squeezing together the bottom of the slider's wings with pliers. Crimp the top and bottom halves on both sides together slightly, testing the zipper before crimping again. If this doesn't work, you'll need to install a new one.

To do this, first remove the defective slider by using pliers to carefully pull off the stop at the bottom on the zipper. A closed-end zipper (meaning one sewn together at the bottom) will have to be opened by removing the stitching. Be careful not to tear the zipper tape. Now you can slip the broken slider off the bottom of the zipper.

Next, slide the wide end of the new slider onto each side of the zipper. Push the slider upward so that each side of the zipper is even with the other; continue until several rows of teeth are locked below the slider. Hold both sides of the zipper together and slowly work the zipper up and down to ensure that the zipper is even and there is no buckling.

Finally, replace the zipper stop, or sew in a makeshift one. To do this, thread a needle with 18 inches of thread, and tie the ends together. Stitch loops through the zipper tape between the bottom two teeth until you've built up enough thread to stop the slider. If repairing a closed-end zipper, stitch the zipper back into the fabric.

—DAVID DRAPER

48 PACK FOR CAMPING IN 5 MINUTES

Plan your fun: Designate three large plastic storage bins and two large laundry bags for camping gear. Store the tent in one laundry bag and the sleeping bags in the other. In one bin, store air mattresses, pumps, pillows, and tarps. In another, pack up stoves, pots and pans, lanterns, hatchets, rope, saws, and other camp tools. Keep the third bin stocked with items that you'll need for camp and kitchen: a small bag of favorite spices, toilet paper, paper towels, camp soap, spare rope, the first aid kit, and the like. Resist the temptation to raid the bins when you're at home and down to your last paper towel. That way, when you're heading out for camp, all you have to do is load the bins and bags, and your work is half done. And once at camp the empty bins serve as great dirty laundry hampers and dry storage for firewood until it's time to pack up and head home. —T.E.N.

49 PIPE WATER FROM A SPRING TO CAMP

Everyone wants a camp in the woods, but nobody wants to haul water. Locate your cabin or base camp downhill from a spring, and you can pipe water to where you need it.

Punch holes in the bottom of a jug and up one side (a). Wrap the jug with a filter of clean cloth and secure with cord (b). Then cut a hole in the cap just large enough to insert tubing (c). Next, seal around the tubing with a silicone-based sealant. Place the jug in the spring with its mouth facing downhill (d). Anchor it with a log.

Run the tubing into a collecting bucket. Don't forget to purify water collected in the wild. —T.E.N.

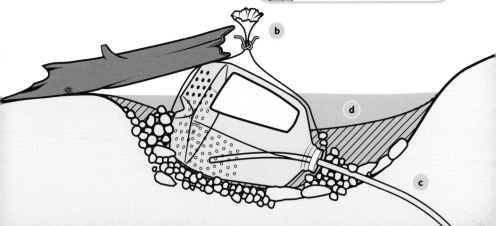

50 MAKE SOAP FROM FIRE

Did you forget soap for washing your camp dishes? Never fear, you can make some from the ashes of your campfire. Just scoop a handful of ashes into a used cookpot (one you've cooked meat or something fatty in), along with a few hot coals. Then dribble in a little bit of water, mixing with a stick to form a thin paste. This produces a rudimentary form of lye which, when mixed with leftover grease, makes basic soap. Just note this concoction can irritate your skin and eyes. —K.M.

51 KEEP YOUR COOLER COLD TWICE AS LONG

Cut a piece of cardboard or minicell foam to fit inside the top of each of your coolers. These disposable gaskets will seal in the cold and make ice last much longer, especially in partially filled coolers. In a pinch, layers of newspaper work like a charm, too. —T.E.N.

52 CRAFT A COOKIE-TIN GRILL

Do you have one of those round cookie tins left over from the holidays? If not, buy one, eat the cookies, and keep the tin, because you can turn it into a great compact camping grill. Simply fill it two-thirds full with match-light barbecue briquettes, close the lid, and stash the tin in your vehicle with your other gear. Once it's time to eat, light the briquettes and place the grate over the top. When the coals are hot enough, place your chops or steaks on the grill. When you're finished, snap the lid back on to smother the coals. Let the tin cool, and it'll be ready for the next grilling session. Just don't let your buddies mistake the briquettes for cookies in the dark. —SAM FADALA

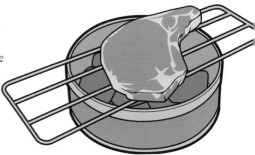

53 SHARPEN A SERRATED BLADE

Think of the blade on a serrated knife as a carnivore's teeth: the sharp points do the killing and receive the wear, while the recessed teeth stay sharp to shave meat from the bone. Designed to maintain an edge, a serrated blade will continue to cut after a fashion even when worn, because the scallops and V notches receive less wear than the points. The catch is that the serrated blade eventually begins to tear and shred rather than slicing cleanly. And that's where the trouble starts, since most people have no idea how to sharpen a blade like this properly. It's not actually that difficult—just keep in mind that you are sharpening only the side of the blade with the serrations. The opposite surface remains flat.

WORK THE ANGLES Hold your sharpener at an angle that matches the original angle of the serrations. The easiest way to do this, and to maintain that angle as you work, is to position your thumb on the back of the blade, resting the edge of the thumb against the hone. To determine the right angle to start with, adjust your thumb until the file aligns with the deepest part of the serration.

GET SHARP Place the serration nearest the finger guard into the thin end of the cone-shaped hone. Push or pull the serration into the cone, working toward the thicker end, until the width of the serration is barely filled by the cone. Rotate the sharpener for a consistent result. Repeat this process with that same serration, counting strokes and stopping every few to feel for a raised burr on the flat side of the blade. This burr indicates that the serration is fully sharpened. When you feel it, move on to the next serration, which should require the same number of strokes.

FLIP OVER After you have sharpened all the serrations, flip the knife over. Using very light pressure, grind the burrs off. You can use the diamond hone, but it's best to use a ceramic rod or fine steel that will remove the burr without sacrificing too much metal.

—K.M.

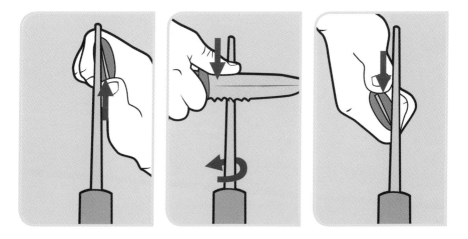

54 TIE A TRUCKER'S HITCH

It's far better to learn how to tie a few knots with (literally) your eyes closed than to kinda-sorta know a bunch. Here is one to add to the basics—the trucker's hitch. This knot will secure a canoe to a car, tighten a tarp, and truss a dozen rods into a tidy bundle. It's one of the best knots out there.

STEP 1 Tie a quick-release loop above any tie-down point, such as a canoe rack.

STEP 2 Run the end of the line around the tie-down and back up through the quick-release loop.

STEP 3 Cinch it down tight and finish with two half hitches.

STEP 4 Pull to tighten. —T.E.N.

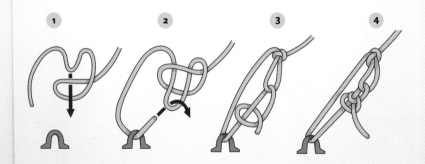

55 ROCK THE PERFECT CAMP STORY

All good stories begin with a variation of "This is no bull," followed by "There we were..." It is essential that you cultivate an ally who will back up your stories in return for your supporting his. You may have no idea what the hell he's talking about, but if your ally says that the deer was 300 yards away when he took the shot and asks for confirmation, you say: "It was every inch of 300 yards. I'd say closer to 350." Your ally, in return, will help you push the deer that got away well into the Pope and Young Club category.

THE WEATHER SHOULD BE MISERABLE For hunting, arctic is preferred: well below freezing, winds strong enough to bend trees nearly horizontal. For fishing, think equatorial: above 90 degrees F, merciless sun and oppressive humidity, without even a single breath of wind.

ACT RELUCTANT TO TELL YOUR BEST YARNS Remember: Stories are what you tell about yourself; legends are the stories others tell when you're not around. When someone other than your ally says, "Tell these guys about the time you had to hang upside down from a limb to get a clear bow shot at that monster muley in Utah," you'll know you have achieved immortality. —B.H.

56 SPLIT LOGS THE SMART WAY

Splitting firewood doesn't require the strength of an ogre. But whale away without a plan, and you will generate more body heat than campfire BTUs.

FORGET THE AXE Use a 6- to 8-pound maul, erring on the light side—velocity matters more than mass. Dulling the edge slightly prevents it from sticking in the wood. Set up a chopping block. Get a hard surface under the log. Otherwise the ground will absorb the blow.

THINK BEFORE YOU STRIKE Look for splits in the log that extend from the center outward, or other cracks in the end grain. Exploit these weaknesses first. Otherwise, aim your first blows toward the barked edge of the round. It's easier to extract the blade with a rocking motion if it's on the edge. Use your next blows to walk the split across the round.

AIM LOW Strike as if the first 3 or 4 inches of wood don't exist. Visualize the maul moving all the way through the wood. Make every swing count. —T.E.N.

57 TEST GEAR IN THE STORE

What can 5 minutes of serious study tell you about the gear you're about to buy? Plenty, if you take advantage of these in-store gear tests. Just ignore the stares of other shoppers, and think twice about buying from a store that won't let you put its products through these paces.

SLEEPING BAG Take off your shoes, spread the bag on a cot or the store floor, and climb in. Sit up in the bag and try to touch your toes. If it binds you, opt for a longer size. Next, lie back down. Zip the bag open and closed three times from the inside, and three times from the outside. If the zipper hangs up on the zipper tape or draft tube, keep looking.

BOOTS Shop in the late afternoon when your feet will have swollen up as much as they're going to over the course of a day. Be sure to wear the sock combination you prefer in the field. Put them on, and then lean forward slightly. Slide your index finger between your heel and the inside of the boot. There shouldn't be much more than a half-inch gap. Next,

kick the wall. If your toes rub or bump the front of the boot, tie the laces a bit tighter, and try again. Still bumping? Keep shopping.

DAYPACK Load the proposed pack with a volume similar to a typical day's worth of hunting or fishing gear, stuff one more spare vest inside, and sling it on. Raise your arms overhead to make sure the sternum strap doesn't cut across your throat. Hip belts should ride on the hips, not above the navel. Rock your shoulders back and forth—if loose webbing flies around, you can be sure it will catch on branches.

FLASHLIGHT First make sure you can manipulate all settings while wearing gloves. Headlamps, in particular, tend to have small switches. Next, tape a piece of unlined white paper to the wall of the store's changing room or bathroom, and turn off the light (if possible). Look for a bright central spot beam with enough spill—light around the edges—to illuminate the sides of a trail. Dark spots and circles show on the paper? Grab a different light. —T.E.N.

58 WIELD A FIELD WRENCH

Can't get a rusty bolt loose? This trick will help. Wrap parachute cord tightly around the nut counterclockwise, leaving a tag end that's long enough for you to wrap around your hand and grasp firmly. Then, start pulling! That ought to do it.
—T.E.N.

59 DIG A BOOTY HOLE

So it's not exactly what you're thinking. For a more comfortable night in your sleeping bag, dig a "hip hollow" or "booty hole" before pitching the tent. Dig or tamp down a slight depression in the ground—a couple inches is plenty—where your pelvis will rest once you lie down. If you sleep on your back, the hole relieves painful pressure points at the small of your back. If you're a side sleeper, your hip will nestle into the hole, keeping your spine aligned for a more restful snooze. —T.E.N.

60 COOK A MEAN BANNOCK

Bannock is easy to make, infinitely customizable, and delicious. Some folks fry it, but if you bake it, it comes out suffused with wood smoke and history.

STEP 1 Put flour, baking powder, nonfat dry milk, oil, and salt into a bowl. Mix. Knead in enough water to make thick dough.

STEP 2 Toss in whatever goodies are handy, such as raisins, berries, jam, honey, cinnamon, or pemmican bits.

STEP 3 Make a pizzalike bannock cake no thicker than $1/2$ inch. Heat a little oil in an iron skillet with straight sides. Fry the bannock on low heat for a few minutes until firm.

STEP 4 Prop the pan on a stick at a 45-degree angle beside the campfire. After 10 minutes, rotate the pan 180 degrees and bake 10 to 15 minutes more. Dig in. —T.E.N

INGREDIENTS

2 cups flour
2 tsp. baking powder
1 tbsp. nonfat dry milk
5 tbsp. oil, melted butter, or lard
Pinch of salt
$1^{1}/_{2}$ cups water (more or less as needed)
Raisins or other additives (optional)

61 CATCH FISH AT YOUR CAMPSITE

In many parts of the country, bush hooking is a revered tradition. Using small boats and canoes, anglers rig a number of setlines to limbs overhanging the stream. For hunters and anglers camping on or near moving water, a bush hook is a fine way to fill a frying pan while attending to camp chores or chasing other fish and game. (Remember: You should check local regulations concerning unattended lines.)

Start by finding a stout sapling or limb that extends over the water a few feet upstream of a desired fishing location. Good bets are strong eddy lines, tributary outfalls, and deep holes beneath undercut banks. To set up the bush hook, attach a three-way swivel to 30- to 50-pound monofilament. Tie one dropper line to an egg sinker and another to the hook. Fasten the main line to the sapling or branch, load the hook with a bait that will hold up to strong current—cut bait, live shiners, shrimp—and drop it into the water. You'll want to check it every couple of hours. And be sure to remove it when you break camp. —T.E.N.

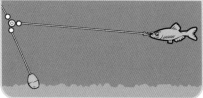

62 FIX ANY TEAR, RIP, OR FRAY

Seam sealers are the best glues you've never heard of. Sure, the stuff waterproofs tent and tarp seams, but a urethane-based sealer also provides a flexible, waterproof, wear-resistant film that can save many a garment. Check out these uses.

WATERPROOF SYNTHETIC GUNSTOCKS Run a bed of seam sealer around butt pads and the threads of connecting screws. This will prevent water from leaking into hollow stocks.

REPAIR RAINCOAT RIPS Close the tear, using tape on the inside of the coat. Brush seam sealer on the outside, covering 1/8 inch on each side of the rip. Let it cure according to manufacturer's directions and then repeat the sealing step on the inside.

KEEP ROPES FROM FRAYING Use seam sealer to permanently whip-finish the ends of ropes and cords. —T.E.N.

HOLDING THE KNIFE

Hold the knife by the back of its blade, with the edge facing out, so that you don't cut your hand. Keep your wrist stiff throughout the throwing motion.

63 TURN A CANOE INTO A CAMPSITE (ALMOST)

Sure, a canoe hauls mountains of gear, puts you in the fish, and floats out the biggest bucks with ease. But don't turn your back on this ancient craft once you get to shore. With a few tricks, that boat can make camp life a lot easier—and it could save your life.

CAMP TABLE AND KITCHEN COUNTER Properly stabilized, a canoe makes a fine table for food preparation. Turn the boat upside down on level ground. Wedge rocks or logs under the bow and stern to prevent the canoe from tipping and wobbling. Now you have a rock-steady flat surface ready for a camp stove, wash bucket, and lantern. You can even fillet fish on the hull and let tomorrow's miles wash away the slime and guts.

WINDBREAK FOR FIRE Canoe campsites are often exposed on sandbars, gravel flats, islands, and windy shorelines. Turn a boat on one edge and prop it up with a pair of sticks to blunt fire-sucking winds.

EMERGENCY SHELTER A canoe can do double duty as a lifesaving shelter when the weather goes south. Turn the canoe upside down and prop one end on a low, sturdy tree branch, a boulder, or—in a pinch—a mound of gear. The high end of the canoe should be pointing away from the wind. Drape a tarp or emergency space blanket over the hull and stake down the edges. Crawl inside and wait out the weather. —T.E.N.

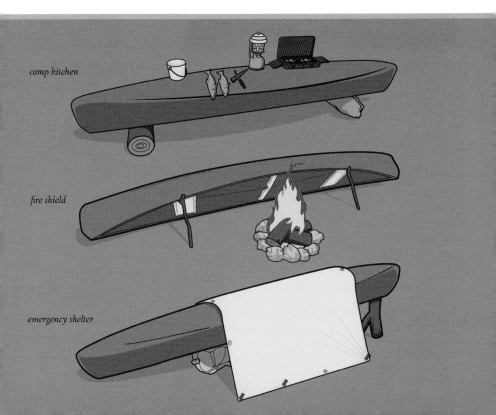

64 THROW A KNIFE

Throwing a knife isn't difficult once you learn how to gauge the speed of rotation. Special throwing knives are unsharpened and have metal handles, but with practice—and caution—you can throw a hunting knife. Three tips: Keep your wrist stiff, use the same speed and motion for each throw, and step toward or away from the target until you find the distance where the rotation turns the knife point-first. Experts can accurately gauge up to seven rotations, but start with one and a half. This will result in a point-first direction with about a 4-yard throw. —K.M.

camp kitchen

fire shield

emergency shelter

65 OPEN A BEER WITH A DOLLAR

Got a dollar? You can use it to drink a beer! And we're not talking about the PBR specials at your local honky-tonk. No, this is another crazy way to pop the cap of your brew with nary a can opener in sight.

STEP 1 Fold the dollar in half, and crease the fold.

STEP 2 Tightly toll the bill up, then bend the rolled bill in half.

STEP 3 Crook your index finger and hold the rolled bill in place with thumb on top, the fold barely sticking over the edge of your knuckle.

STEP 4 Place the fold of the bill under the bottle cap. Push upwards.

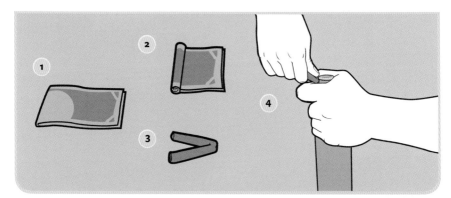

66 STUFF A DUFFLE

After a day or two of camping, a cavernous duffle bag devolves into a jumbled morass of clothing and equipment. Stop wasting your time rooting through this mess and get organized.

First, buy some inexpensive stuff sacks in various colors and sizes, one for each different type of item you're packing: shirts, pants, rain gear, socks, underwear, etc. Then roll your clothing into tubes the length of the designated sack, and just slide them in. Half a dozen shirts will fit in a medium sack.

Pack smaller pieces of spare gear such as headlamps, spare cartridges, and extra batteries in clear plastic resealable bags.

Now stuff your monstrous duffle with these smaller sacks, and you'll never spend another minute wondering where you put your favorite long underwear. Your color-coded system will help you locate what you want. Retrieving it is as simple as pulling the rolled-up garment free while everything else stays in place—it's like removing a Vienna sausage from a can.

67 TIE A KNUTE HITCH

Simplicity itself, the Knute hitch is perfect for tying a lanyard to the holes in knife handles and other essential tools.

STEP 1 Start by tying an overhand stopper knot in one end of the cord. Thread a loop through the lanyard hole, and push the stopper knot up through it.

STEP 2 Snug it tight, and you are done. —T.E.N.

68 COOK THE CAMPER'S SUCKLING PIG

Cavemen cooked large hunks of meat on sticks—at least in cartoons—but what did they care if it took a couple hundred thousand years to char a mammoth leg? Too often, you're too beat to go into an *Iron Chef* smackdown gourmet extravaganza after a day of slogging through duck swamps. You want *hot meat now*. Sausages are perfect for roasting over a fire. The trick lies in cooking them sl-o-o-o-w, so they can cook all the way through without scorching on the outside. Cut a green branch and sharpen the tip.

Build a good bed of coals and hold the skewer 6 inches over the coals, rotating frequently. The sausage is done when the juices run clear.

If a kebab is what you're craving, slice the sausage into inch-thick chunks and rehydrate a few sun-dried tomatoes and dehydrated mushrooms. Skewer the goodies and cook them over a hot fire. Beats ramen noodles every time.

Mmmm...juicy. Skewered meat and fire is as basic as it gets. It's just about as delicious as it gets, too. —T.E.N.

69 CHOOSE THE IDEAL SITE FOR YOUR WILDERNESS CAMP

Location, location, location: Choosing the right site out in the deep wilderness is easy enough, if you just keep a few factors in mind. For maximum comfort, you'll want a flat, soft forest floor. Even a slight incline can make for major discomfort once you lay down to sleep. Spongy duff (decaying leaves and branches) makes a soft mattress, and also absorbs any rain or snowmelt, helping to keep you dry.

TREE TIPS Find a spot with enough trees that you'll have shade when you need it, as well as stable anchor points. That said, be sure you're not near dead trees, or trees with big limbs that might break off in a high wind. Finally, beware of tall, tapering trees that might draw lightning strikes.

WATER WISDOM It's ideal to be near a source of clear water, but not too close—the deep draw around a creek can be 15 degrees colder than surrounding areas at night. Never pitch camp in a gully that shows signs of flash flooding, or under cliffs or avalanche chutes.

BE EARTH FRIENDLY Don't camp on delicate leafy plants or alpine vegetation. The environmentally correct thing to do is to choose sand, small gravel, dry grass, or even hard-packed earth, if you must. And remember that in some wilderness areas, it's illegal to camp near a lake, stream, or major trail. —K.M.

70 START SNORING BEFORE YOUR BUNKMATE

When it comes to catching some Z's in the backwoods, nothing is worse than racing a bunkmate to see who can fall asleep first, before the heavy timber-cutting begins. In this case the best defense is a good offense (and sometimes slightly offensive).

A TOAST Offer him a nightcap, a nice rum-and-soda . . . with Red Bull!

FALSE ALARM Turn his cell phone to vibrate and set the alarm to go off half an hour after lights-out. Once he figures out what's making the fuss, he'll have a hard time reentering dreamland.

SCRATCHERS GAME Slip a few local samples of scratchy materials into his sleeping bag. Maple seeds, cockleburs, sand spurs, and toenail clippings work.

71 TOAST GRILLED CHEESE ON A STICK

This is a fun way for kids to cook themselves a somewhat familiar treat... and get something healthy in their stomachs before the inevitable s'mores. And, of course, if you had a bad day hunting or fishing, you might join them for a sammich or two!

PREP YOUR STICK Find yourself a good sturdy stick that has a natural "Y" in it, and peel the bark from the spot where your sandwich will sit.

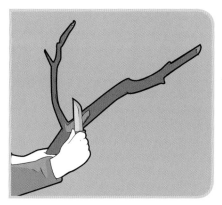

BUTTER UP Take two slices of bread and butter them well, then add a few slices of cheese to make a sandwich.

GET TOASTY Place your sandwich on the stick and grill carefully over your campfire.

FLIP OUT Remove from fire, flip over.

TOAST IT UP Grill the other side until your sandwich is a nice crispy brown and filled with delicious melty cheese. Enjoy! Hey, you almost don't miss that fish that got away now, do you?

72 HANG OUT IN A HAMMOCK

There are few things as relaxing as swinging free in your hammock at the end of a long day...and few things as embarrassing as falling on your ass in front of all your hunting buddies trying to get into the darn thing. Follow these simple steps and you never need to be embarrassed again... about this, anyway.

STEP 1 Spread the netting with your hands to create your "landing point" right at the center of the hammock.

STEP 2 Sit carefully back into the area you've prepped.

STEP 3 Swing your bent legs up into the hammock in one swoop.

STEP 4 Lay back and relax.

STEP 5 For power napping and all-night dozing, sleep on an angle—it's the most stable position.

73 TRACK BACK WITH A GPS

Most people use a handheld GPS as little more than a fancy compass, but in fact it can be an awesome tool for hunters, fishermen, and campers looking to plot a trail from trailhead, truck, or campsite and back. Here's how to do it right:

STEP 1 Turn the GPS unit on, leave it on, and leave it out where it can get a clear signal.

STEP 2 Activate the track-log function (this goes by different names with different units, such as "Tracks" for Garmin devices, or "Trails" for Magellan.) Don't customize the settings, such as how often the unit plots a waypoint—the auto mode is best for your purposes, as it will change the timing of waypoints based on how fast you're moving.

STEP 3 At your final destination, stop the track log and store the name of the track before powering off. You can now easily follow that track back the way you came with your unit's return feature.

74 CRAP LIKE A CAT

Only a pure jackass leaves toilet paper on the ground. Dealing with human waste in the woods is easy. Do it right every time by burying your poop in a cathole.

STEP 1 Select a spot at least 70 paces from the nearest water source. Open sun is best because it speeds decomposition. Use the heel of your boot to kick out a hole 6 to 8 inches deep and 4 to 6 inches in diameter.

STEP 2 No need for details about this step.

STEP 3 Use a stick to mix your output with soil to give decomposing bacteria a jump start.

STEP 4 Deal with the toilet paper. According to the organization Leave No Trace, "burying toilet paper in a cathole is not generally recommended." That leaves three choices: Carry it out (can you say double-wrap?); burn it (with a stick, put all the used toilet paper in the cathole, ignite it, and then fill the cathole with water); or bury it anyway—just tamp it down in the bottom of the cathole.

STEP 5 Fill the hole with dirt and camouflage it with leaves and brush. It takes 30 seconds to render a cathole invisible. —T.E.N.

75 TIE A CLOVE HITCH

The clove hitch is the foundational knot for many pole-lashing techniques, including the tripod pictured at right. It's also a great basic boating knot, useful for a temporary stay to a dock or piling. —T.E.N.

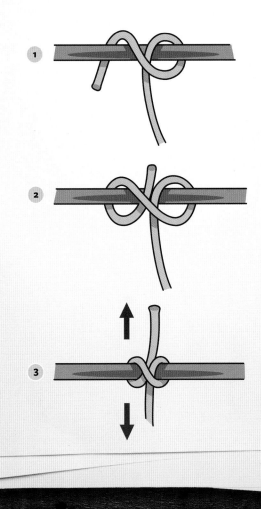

76 MAKE A WATER BOWL FOR YOUR DOG

Your best friend needs his water, especially out on a long hike or an all-day hunt. Sure you can buy all kinds of fancy collapsible dog bowls, but there's no need to spend all that money. To make a handy lightweight bowl, cut off the bottom third of an empty gallon jug. Then take another jug and fill it with water. The "bowl" will fit snugly over the bottom of the jug, which makes it convenient to bring both the water and the bowl along when you and Fido head out on the trail.

77 LASH A TRIPOD

Suspending a kettle over your campfire lets you cook up stew, boil water, and otherwise expand your campsite options. With three poles and some cord, you're well on your way.

STEP 1 Place three poles on the ground with the center pole facing away from the other two.

STEP 2 Tie a clove hitch on the left pole (see left for instructions).

STEP 3 Wrap the cord seven times over, under, and around the poles. Finish it off by lashing the rope between the poles, and finish with another clove hitch.

STEP 4 Raise the tripod; this will automatically tighten the lashings. Settle it over the fire, hang your kettle, and get started on your squirrel casserole!

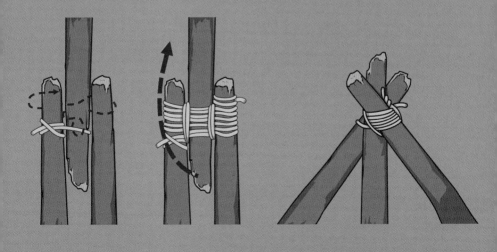

78 PADDLE A SOLO CANOE LIKE A CHAMP

Can you really rock out some speed in a canoe all by yourself? You sure can if you follow these hints from three-time Outdoorsman Challenge winner and canoe maestro Paul Thompson:

GO BACKWARD Try turning your boat around and paddling from behind the center thwart, which will distribute your weight across the widest part of the canoe.

GET LOW AND LEAN Kneeling slightly off-center keeps your center of gravity low and means that your paddle is closer to the water than when you're sitting upright. A slight lean gives the boat a long, keel-like profile, which can make a huge difference in how it handles.

CHOP CHOP Short strokes are the best way to get the canoe moving. Attack that water like Paul Bunyan with a caffeine buzz!

79 ENHANCE YOUR DEER CAMP EXPERIENCE

In addition to the absolute basics, here are a few more things that will make your life in deer camp even more enjoyable than it already is. Bet you didn't think that was possible.

SMALL FLASHLIGHT If you wear it on a lanyard, you'll always know right where it is.

MULTITOOL Good for everything from slicing cheese to fixing lanterns.

CAMP SHOES Rubber-soled, for those midnight trips from your tent out to water the perimeter.

BABY WIPES Much better than TP in a no-shower situation, especially by day four. Just make sure you don't let the other guys see them.

RUBBER TOTE Keep your hunting clothes from smelling like smoke, grease, or worse.

FOAM EARPLUGS One of your campmates may snore loudly enough to be heard across the campsite.

ASPIRIN Bring this in case you wake up with a headache after a late night by the fire. Hair of the dog isn't an option when you're planning on going hunting that day. —LAWRENCE PYNE

80 FOLD A TOPO MAP

A 7.5-minute guide or 1:24 topographic map is the backcountry hunter's guide to public-land gold, but it's typically sold one of only two ways: flat or rolled in a tube. Neither of these storage styles will allow it to fit in your pack, but you don't have to be an origami expert to make it pocket friendly. Just follow the steps below. Once you're finished, you can use the creases as guides to fold the map in a convenient way that shows just the area you're navigating.

WEST MEETS EAST Lay the map face up in front of you with the name in the upper-right hand corner. Make a vertical fold in the middle of the map by bringing the left (west) edge over to the right (east) edge. Crease this, and all other folds, tightly by running your finger along it.

QUARTERED BORDERS Fold the western edge of the map back toward the crease you just made in Step 1. Then, flip the map over and repeat with the eastern edge. The topographic map should now be folded in vertical quarters, and the name of the map should be at the top.

NORTH TO SOUTH Grasp the north edge and make a horizontal fold in the middle as you bring it down to meet the south. Fold the north edge back to the crease you just created. Flip the map and repeat. Keep your perfectly folded topographic map protected in a quart-size zip-seal bag. —DAVID DRAPER

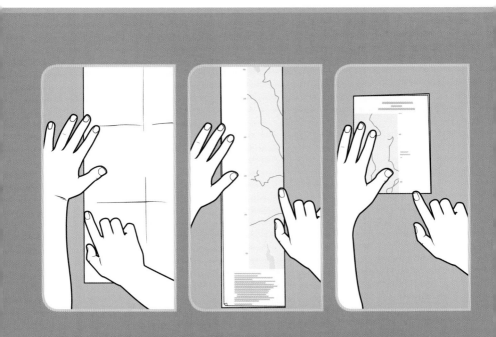

81 KEEP PARACHUTE CORD TANGLE-FREE

Parachute cord is the camper and hunter's best friend for so many reasons (from serving as emergency shoelaces to letting you saw through all sorts of substances). But it can be an unholy mess if it gets tangled—and it always gets tangled. The best way to store your precious paracord is in an empty peanut-butter jar. To do this, first drill a ³⁄₁₆-inch-diameter hole in the lid. Stuff the cord into the jar, being careful not to overlap it onto itself. Then thread about 4 inches of cord through the hole you made. Screw the lid back on, dispense cord as you need it, and kiss tangles good-bye.

82 STAY WARM WITH A SPACE BLANKET

The space blanket, a lightweight mylar sheet common to any good survival kit, is a great multiuse product, and shouldn't be saved for the unlikely event that you need to keep from freezing to death in the Alaskan tundra (although if it does come to that, you'll be glad of the blanket, that's for sure!). Try placing one under your tent for insulation, or wrapping it over your sleeping bag. In a pinch, you can even use it as a drop-cloth for dressing game! —K.M.

83 SMUDGE OUT CAMPSIDE SKEETERS

In our high-stakes chemical warfare against mosquitoes, we often forget the simplest insect repellant . . . smoke. As your campfire burns down, collect moss, punky wood, leafy boughs, grass, and as much bark as you can peel from deadfall evergreens. If you can find wood that contains natural repellents such as sage or cedar, all the better. Once you have a deep, glowing bed of coals, pile on the green. Fan it with your hat to get it going, and enjoy a bite-free evening. —K.M.

84 WASH CAMP DISHES IN RECORD TIME

Sure, that big pot of stew was just what you wanted after a long day's hunt . . . but now the guys are opening beers and starting the poker game, and you're stuck on dish duty. To avoid wasting precious drinking and campfire story time, you need to plan ahead. Next time, heat a fair amount of water over the fire or campstove, and presoak all the pots and pans as soon as they're emptied. Then fill two dishpans with hot water. Add biodegradable dish soap to one for cleaning, use the other for rinsing. To make life even easier, just use paper plates, and burn after using. —L.P.

85 OPEN WINE CAVEMAN STYLE

Who brings a bottle of wine to a deer camp? You'd be surprised...not every hunter is a beer-and-chips kinda guy—some of us actually enjoy a nice red wine with our venison. But when you forget the corkscrew? That's when you need to get in touch with your inner caveman.

FOILED AGAIN Remove the foil from the top of the bottle with your camping knife.

WRAP IT UP Wrap the bottle in a towel, heavy jacket, or other good, strong padding.

WHACK IT GOOD Thump the butt of the bottle repeatedly against a tree, with the bottle angled slightly downwards. The force of the wine and the air inside the bottle will begin to force the cork out a bit.

GRAB AND PULL When the cork starts to emerge, you should be able to grab it with your hand and pull it out. Now pour yourself a nice tin cup of cabernet and get back to those steaks!

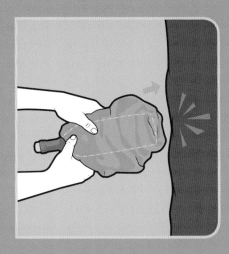

86 MAKE A TARP TEPEE

Maybe you were planning to sleep under the stars but suddenly the rain started falling. Maybe your tentmate snores so loudly you had to strike out on your own. Whatever the reason, sometimes you need to make a shelter in a hurry. Here's a handy trick that'll get you through the night warm, dry, and snore-free.

STEP 1 Unfold your tarp and place a rock in the middle.

STEP 2 Grab a length of rock and tie a knot to keep the rock in place.

STEP 3 Sling the other end of the rope over a nice sturdy branch.

STEP 4 Raise your tarp up as high as you like, then tie the other end of the rope off to the trunk.

STEP 5 Spread the base of your tarp out to make a tepee and then anchor the edges with rocks. Alternatively—if you don't mind damaging your tarp a bit— you can drive tent pegs right through it.

STEP 6 Add leaves for insulation if you don't have a big enough sleeping pad. Crawl inside and get that rest you so richly deserve!

87 CAMP LIKE A GHOST

GET IN Good campsites are found, not made. Don't clear brush for your tent or dig drainage ditches. Stick to existing fire circles in heavily used areas. Otherwise, plan to camouflage the fire pit by shoveling out a layer of soil and surface plants and setting it aside. And no surveyor's tape for flagging. Learn to use a map and compass or a GPS.

GET OUT Burn all wood completely. Saturate the ashes and then scatter them. Replace the sod and toss leaves and twigs over the spot. Scour the camp for tiny bits of micro-trash. Remove all cordage from trees, even if you didn't place it there. Naturalize the site before you leave. Rake matted grasses and leaves with a branch. Bring in rocks and sticks to hide your tent site. And the same rule applies no matter how near to or far from civilization you camp: Pack it in; pack it out. Yes, that means banana peels, apple cores, eggshells, and cigar butts. If it wasn't there when Columbus landed, remove it. —T.E.N.

RESOURCES

(a) Benchmade Activator +
www.benchmade.com

(b) Spyderco Gayle Bradley
Carbon Fiber Folder
www.spyderco.com

(c) Case Ridgeback
www.wrcase.com

(d) SOG Toothlock Black TiNi
www.sogknives.com

(e) Buck Special
www.buckknives.com

(f) Lone Wolf Trailmate
www.lonewolfknives.com

(g) DiamondBlade Pinnacle I
www.diamondbladeknives.com

(h) CRKT Big Eddy II
www.crkt.com

FIELD & STREAM

In every issue of *Field & Stream* you'll find a lot of stuff: beautiful photography and artwork, adventure stories, wild game recipes, humor, commentary, reviews, and more. That mix is what makes the magazine so great, what's helped it remain relevant since 1895. But at the heart of every issue are the skills. The tips that explain how to land a big trout, the tactics that help you shoot the deer of your life, the lessons that teach you how to survive a cold night outside—those are the stories that readers have come to expect from *Field & Stream*.

You'll find a ton of those skills in this book, but there's not a book big enough to hold them all in one volume. Besides, whether you're new to hunting and fishing or an old pro, there's always more to learn. You can continue to expect *Field & Stream* to teach you those essential skills in every issue. Plus, there's all that other stuff in the magazine, too, which is pretty great. To order a subscription, visit www.fieldandstream.com/subscription.

FIELDANDSTREAM.COM

When *Field & Stream* readers aren't hunting or fishing, they kill hours (and hours) on www.fieldandstream.com. And once you visit the site, you'll understand why. If you enjoy the skills in this book, there's plenty more online—both within our extensive archives of stories from the writers featured here, as well as our network of 50,000-plus experts who can answer all of your questions about the outdoors.

At Fieldandstream.com, you'll get to explore the world's largest online destination for hunters and anglers. Our blogs, written by the leading experts in the outdoors, cover every facet of hunting and fishing and provide constant content that instructs, enlightens, and always entertains. Our collection of adventure videos contains footage that's almost as thrilling to watch as it is to experience for real. And our photo galleries include the best wildlife and outdoor photography you'll find anywhere. Perhaps best of all is the community you'll find at Fieldandstream.com. It's where you can argue with other readers about the best whitetail cartridge or the perfect venison chili recipe. It's where you can share photos of the fish you catch and the game you shoot. It's where you can enter contests to win guns, gear, and other great prizes. And it's a place where you can spend a lot of time. Which is OK. Just make sure to reserve some hours for the outdoors, too.

THE TOTAL OUTDOORSMAN CHALLENGE

If you enjoyed this book, we encourage you to check out the book it was excerpted from, *The Total Outdoorsman*. This collection of 374 skills covering Camping, Fishing, Hunting, and Survival will make you a true outdoors expert. You'll be ready to take on the world—or at least the wild. Go for it. But you might also consider displaying your newly acquired skills in another arena: the Total Outdoorsman Challenge.

Since 2004, *Field & Stream* has ventured on an annual countrywide search for the nation's best all-around outdoorsman—the person who's equally competent with a rifle, shotgun, bow, rod, and paddle, the person who can do it all. And whoever proves he can do it all walks away with the Total Outdoorsman title, as well as tens of thousands of dollars in cash and prizes.

The Total Outdoorsman Challenge is about more than hunting and fishing, though. The event celebrates our belief that the more outdoor skills you have, the more fun you can have in the woods and on the water. It celebrates the friendships that can only happen between sportsmen. Every year thousands of sportsmen compete in the Total Outdoorsman Challenge, and every year many of those competitors meet new hunting and fishing buddies.

So, once you're ready, you should consider testing your skills in the Total Outdoorsman Challenge. (Visit www.totaloutdoorsmanchallenge.com to learn more about the event.) And if you're not sure you're quite ready, you can always read the book again.

INDEX

ACKNOWLEDGMENTS

From the Author, T. Edward Nickens
I would like to thank all of the talented people
who made this book possible, including the *Field
& Stream* staff editors who guided this project
with great care and insight. *Field & Stream* field
editors Phil Bourjaily, Keith McCafferty, John
Merwin, and David E. Petzal, and editor-at-large
Kirk Deeter, provided unmatched expertise. Just
good enough is never good enough for them. I
wish I could name all the guides, outfitters, and
hunting, fishing, and camping companions I've
enjoyed over the years. Every trip has been a
graduate course in outdoor skills, and much of
the knowledge within the covers of this book I've
learned at the feet of others. And last, thanks to
my longtime field partner, Scott Wood, who has
pulled me out of many a bad spot, and whose
skillful, detailed approach to hunting and fishing
is an inspiration.

From *Field & Stream*'s Editor,
Anthony Licata
I would like to thank Weldon Owen publisher
Roger Shaw, executive editor Mariah Bear, and
art director Iain Morris, who have put together a
book filled with skills that have stood the test of
time—in a package that should do the same. I'd
also like to thank Eric Zinczenko, *Field & Stream*
VP and Group Publisher, for championing the
Total Outdoorsman concept in all its forms. This
great collection of skills would not have been
possible without the hard work of the entire *Field
& Stream* team, and I'd particularly like to thank
Art Director Sean Johnston, Photo Editor Amy
Berkley, former Art Director Neil Jamieson,
Executive Editor Mike Toth, Managing Editor
Jean McKenna, Deputy Editor Jay Cassell,
Senior Editor Colin Kearn, and Associate Editor
Joe Cermele. I'd also like to thank Sid Evans
for his role in creating the Total Outdoorsmen
concept. Finally, I'd like to thank my father,
Joseph Licata, who first brought me into the
fields and streams and showed me what being a
total outdoorsman really meant.

CREDITS

Cover images Front: Shutterstock (flashlight,
background texture) Back: Left, Raymond
Larette Center, Hayden Foell Right, Lauren
Towner

Photography courtesy of Shutterstock, with
the following exceptions: Cliff Gardiner and
John Keller: 4, 8 (wire saw) iStockphoto: 41, 60
Alexander Ivanov: 40 Spencer Jones: 8 (T-shirt,
portable stove) Pippa Morris: 42 T. Edward
Nickens: Camping introduction (hunter and
child) 37 Travis Rathbone: 18 Dan Saelinger:

Camping introduction (lantern) Dusan Smetana:
Camping introduction (tent) 55

Illustrations courtesy of Conor Buckley: 52,
65, 77, 80, 81 flying-chilli.com: 16 Hayden Foell:
14, 86 Alan Kikuchi: icon of tent Raymond
Larett: 11, 13, 61 Daniel Marsiglio: 3, 29, 31, 32,
45, 49, 53, 63, 64 Will McDermott: 4 Robert L.
Prince: 7, 22, 58 Jameson Simpson: 26 Jeff Soto:
15 Lauren Towner: 19, 39, 33, 54, 67 Tina Cash
Walsh: 71, 72, 85 Paul Williams: 28, 38

CONTRIBUTORS

T. Edward Nickens (T.E.N.) is Editor-at-Large of *Field & Stream* magazine. Known for do-it-yourself wilderness adventures and profiles about people and places where hunting and fishing are the heart and soul of a community, he has chased ptarmigan and char north of the Arctic Circle, antelope in Wyoming, and striped marlin from a kayak in Baja California. He will not turn down any assignment that involves a paddle or a squirrel. Author of the magazine's "Total Outdoorsman" skills features, he also is host, writer, and co-producer for a number of *Field & Stream*'s television and Web shows, among them *The Total Outdoorsman Challenge* and *Heroes of Conservation*. Nickens has been a National Magazine Award finalist, and has won more than 30 writing awards, including three "Best of the Best" top honors awards from the Outdoor Writers Association of America. He lives in Raleigh, North Carolina, within striking distance of mountain trout, saltwater fly fishing, and a beloved 450-acre hunting lease that has been the cause of many a tardy slip for his two school-age children.

Keith McCafferty (K.M.) writes the "Survival" and "Outdoor Skills" columns for *Field & Stream*, and contributes adventure narratives and how-to stories to both the magazine and Fieldandstream.com. McCafferty has been nominated for numerous National Magazine Awards over the years, most recently for his February 2007 cover story, "Survivor." McCafferty's assignments for *Field & Stream* have taken him as far as the jungles of India and as close to home as his back yard. McCafferty lives in Bozeman, Montana, with his wife, Gail. McCafferty loves to fly fish for steelhead in British Columbia and climb the Rockies in pursuit of bull elk.

Additional contributors: David Draper, Sam Fadala, Bill Heavey, Peter B. Mathiesen, and Lawrence Pyne

"*Pair a hunting or fishing trip with a tent and a sleeping bag, or with a deep-woods cabin whose sooty windows are smudged with wood smoke, and every moment seems to be the best there ever was. Every trip is the trip of a lifetime.*"

—T. Edward Nickens

FIELD & STREAM

Editor Anthony Licata

VP, Group Publisher Eric Zinczenko

2 Park Avenue
New York, NY 10016
www.fieldandstream.com

weldon**owen**

President, CEO Terry Newell

VP, Publisher Roger Shaw

Executive Editor Mariah Bear

Creative Director Kelly Booth

Art Director William van Roden

Designer Meghan Hildebrand

Cover Design William Mack

Illustration Coordinator Conor Buckley

Production Director Chris Hemesath

Production Manager Michelle Duggan

All of the material in this book was originally
published in *The Total Outdoorsman: 374 Skills
You Need*, by T. Edward Nickens and the
editors of *Field & Stream*.

Weldon Owen would also like to thank Iain
Morris for the original design concept adapted
from *The Total Outdoorsman*, and Ian Cannon,
Emelie Griffin, Katharine Moore, and Mary
Zhang for editorial assistance.

© 2012 Weldon Owen Inc.

415 Jackson Street
San Francisco, CA 94111
www.weldonowen.com

Field & Stream and Weldon Owen are divisions of
BONNIER

Library of Congress Control Number on file
with the publisher

ISBN 13: 978-1-61628-415-2
ISBN 10: 1-61628-415-3

10 9 8 7 6 5 4 3 2

2013 2014 2015

Printed in China by 1010